INDIA

Land of Dreams and Fantasy

Doranne Jacobson

TODTRI

DEDICATION

THIS BOOK IS DEDICATED TO THE PEOPLE OF INDIA,
WHO MADE IT ALL POSSIBLE.

ACKNOWLEDGMENTS

I would like to express my deep appreciation to the many
people who have helped me to appreciate the complexity of
India's culture and civilization. Among those who have been
particularly helpful in the preparation of this volume are Dr.
Jerome Jacobson, Dr. Owen Lynch, Dr. Suzanne Hanchett,
Dr. John Walthall, Miss Sunalini Nayudu, Mr. Mirza Majid
Hussein Khan, Mrs. Rabiya Sultan Khan, Mr. Roy Moyer, and
Dr. Karl Lunde. I would like to thank these people as well as
Mr. Robert Tod and the photographers whose excellent work
has added so greatly to the beauty of this book.

This book was designed and produced by
Todtri Productions Ltd
P.O. Box 572
New York, NY 10116-0572
Fax: (212) 695-6988

Printed and bound in Korea

ISBN 1–880908–06–9

Author: Doranne Jacobson

Publisher: Robert Tod
Designer and Art Director: Mark Weinberg
Editor: Mary Forsell

Table of Contents

The boundary of India, as depicted here and in other maps of this book, is neither authentic nor correct.

Introduction

Ornamented with loops and circlets of gold, her hair perfumed with jasmine blossoms, and her sari encrusted with fine embroidery, a young woman exemplifies feminine beauty.

India–the land of fantasy and dreams, land of color and variety–the very name makes us think of brilliant silks, bearded holy men, fervent pilgrims, snow–capped peaks, and sacred rivers.

Imagining India, we envision the Taj Mahal's serene white marble dome glowing in the morning mists, and we see a vivid profusion of Hindu deities adorning an elaborate temple tower.

Saffron and silver, pearls and ivory, gold and vermilion all suggest the sumptuous pleasures of India. Images of devout believers immersing themselves in dawn–lit waters or kneeling on thin prayer rugs over hard marble remind us of the spirituality that has distinguished the subcontinent for untold centuries. Parched deserts and palm–fringed beaches, verdant fields and rugged mountain passes, cooling breezes and hot winds all imply the varied nature of India's landscape and climate.

Everywhere amid this kaleidoscopic setting, there are curves and circles, inviting and including, alluring and enclosing. Indian art features spirals and curvaceous lines–vines and tendrils, the globe of the sun, benevolent serpents, round–figured goddesses, circular armlets, oval gemstones, arches and domes, circles of dancers, round–haloed deities, curling elephant trunks, crescent moons, and spiraling conch shells. These representations reflect the all–encompassing nature of Indian culture, which has integrated into its own panoply of customs, philosophies, and materials influences from every corner of the earth to form a uniquely rich and splendid civilization.

India's social complexity and cultural diversity are legendary. The nation's population is the second largest in the world (only China has more people), an incredible mosaic of more than 860 million inhabitants—one-sixth of the world's human beings. They speak fifteen recognized state languages and hundreds of lesser languages and dialects and live in twenty–five states and seven territories flung across a land the size of continental Western Europe. A multitude of ethnic groups, classes, and physical types abound in this great country, the world's largest democracy. India also has social and economic problems of great magnitude, affecting the lives of hundreds of millions of people.

In the streets of the major cities, people of a thousand backgrounds mingle.

The serene beauty of the Taj Mahal shines across the centuries, reflected in the morning mists at Agra, an eternal monument to the love of an emperor for his queen.

Powerful gods and goddesses, including Lord Ganesh, are among the colorful figures adorning a tower of the Meenakshi Temple in Madurai.

At the Pushkar Fair in Rajasthan, high-spirited crowds gather to watch camel racing, tent-pegging, and other robust activities.

Red–turbanned Rajputs and bearded Sikhs rub shoulders with pin–stripe–suited, clean–shaven businessmen and dhoti–clad Brahman priests. Black–veiled Muslim women walk beside sari–draped Hindus. Millionaires reclining in chauffeur–driven cars gaze out their tinted windows at construction laborers bearing headloads of bricks and at pavement vendors hawking their wares. Farmers in homespun shawls and white caps made famous by Gandhi—the ascetic nationalist—gather enthusiastically to buy tickets to see gaudy cinematic dramas starring gold–ornamented dancers and singers. The sonorous tones of the Muslim call to prayer blend with the clang of Hindu temple bells and with lively radio broadcasts of film tunes. From far above, the roar of jet planes piloted by highly educated aviators resound in the ears of illiterate ox–cart drivers.

Riding in the same train car traveling from the North to the South or the East to the West might be a varied mix of passengers: a vegetarian family from Gujarat snacking on oranges, a scholar from Bengal reading poetry, a Bombay grandmother journeying to visit her lawyer son in a distant city, a group of village pilgrims hoping for a glimpse of God's image at a

seashore temple, and a Christian couple journeying to attend a cousin's wedding in a faraway town.

The diversity of India's land and peoples is the country's challenge and its glory. Throughout the centuries and into modern times, within their various ecological zones, India's many religious, ethnic, and regional groups have struggled and cooperated with each other, generating an almost limitless cultural wealth. A great number of groups have sought political and economic power within a small or large domain, and many have achieved their goals, only to face challenges from still other groups striving for preeminence. Differences are always recognized—and somehow, almost always respected. For all of these peoples share a special Indian identity that holds them together, the knowledge that they are all children of the land they call Bharat. They recognize that they are all part of the splendid civilization that has been the creation of all the peoples of this remarkable land.

In sacred circles of carved marble, exquisitely wrought goddesses, nymphs, flowers, and animals adorn a temple's domed ceiling at Mt. Abu. The carvings are so fine the stone seems almost transparent.

A NOTE ON PRONUNCIATION

The Indian words and place names in this book derive from a number of Indian languages. For ease in reading, detailed diacritical marks have not been used, as they would be in a more academic text.

It may be helpful to keep in mind that in Indian words, an "a" is never pronounced as in the English word "cat." Rather, an "a" is pronounced either as a long "ah" sound, such as in English "father," or a short "uh" sound, such as in English "cut." The letter "u" may be pronounced either as in "pull" or in "rule." An "i" may be pronounced as in "pin" or "machine," and an "e" sounds like the vowel in "say." If you would really like to know how to pronounce an Indian word, ask an Indian friend to help you say it correctly.

Nature and History Set the Stage

Indian civilization has grown and flourished within the sheltering embrace of an almost heart–shaped subcontinent, with vast differences in terrain and climate across its length and breadth. Offering a wide variety of ecological conditions, India has nourished a rich complexity of cultural forms, which have developed over the course of many thousands of years.
The land's diversity has affected the many paths taken by the peoples of India throughout prehistory and history, setting the stage for the development of the modern Indian nation.

The Nurturing Landscape

India stretches some 2,000 miles from north to south, and some 1,800 miles from west to east, covering about 1,200,000 square miles—an area approximately one–third the size of the United States. The waters of the Bay of Bengal, the Indian Ocean, and the Arabian Sea wash the subcontinent's sandy shores.

The lofty peaks of the Himalayas—Abode of Snow—shape India's northern boundaries, separating the warmer subcontinent from cold Tibet to the north. Lesser ranges extending out from the Himalayas shield India from Persia and Afghanistan to the west and Burma to the east.

Arising in the snows of the Himalayas, flowing to the south and east, is the mighty Ganges River, known throughout India as Ganga Mai—Mother Ganga—the great source of water for the Indo–Gangetic Plain. Devout Hindus envision it spouting forth from Lord Shiva's head as he sits atop Mt. Meru, the

A village pond in central India is lush with greenery during the wet monsoon season. The annual rains bring welcome moisture to the thirsty land.

Previous Page:
The snowy peaks of the Himalayas shape India's northern boundaries, separating the warmer subcontinent from the colder lands to the north. In Ladakh, a small village lies at the base of the mountains.

force of its fall broken by his long ascetic's tresses. The Ganges is revered throughout India as a goddess and symbolic of the essence of life itself. Seeking spiritual purity, millions of pilgrims bathe in its waters every year. The river plunges tumultuously from its mountainous origin, then flows more slowly across the vast fertile flatlands of North India, bringing essential fluids and silts to the nation's breadbasket.

Far to the west of the Ganges–watered plain lie the desiccated dunes of the Great Indian Desert, where colorfully garbed worshippers must seek out smaller streams and lakes to show their appreciation for the divine gift of water. Farther to the west is the great Indus River and its alluvial plain–now largely in Pakistan, but vital to the rise of India's earliest civilization. In fact, the name "India" was first used by ancient Persians to refer to the land through which the Indus flowed.

High on the Tibetan plateau, melting snows come together in the Brahmaputra River and flow eastward for six hundred miles, finally breaking through the eastern Himalayas into northeastern India. The surging Brahmaputra waters much of India's wet and green far east and the adjacent nation of Bangladesh as well.

Flowing westward across a thousand miles of central India is the sacred Narmada River, bringing nourishment to the forests and farmlands along its course. It cuts through the low–lying Vindhyas and other forested hills, which outline the great division between North and South India.

The huge Deccan (Southern) Plateau extends from the Vindhyas southward for nine hundred miles, flanked by hills and peaks and bordered by fertile green flatlands all along the coasts. The rocky block of the plateau is tilted so that the revered rivers of South India flow predominantly from west to east–the Mahanadi, the Godavari, the Krishna, and the Kaveri.

Interacting with this sacred and nurturing geography are major climatic forces, bringing three primary seasons–cold, hot, and monsoon. The northern mountains shield India from Central Asia's cold; most of the subcontinent enjoys a tropical climate, caressed by warm ocean currents.

The majestic tiger, India's national animal, still roams the forests and fields of isolated areas. These white tigers are descendants of a unique animal raised by the Maharaja of Rewa, formerly the ruler of a small kingdom in central India.

Sambar deer peacefully breakfast on marsh grasses in a lake in one of India's wildlife preserves, reenacting a pageant of timeless natural beauty.

Bombay streets are often flooded during monsoon downpours, and commuters cheerfully cope with the life–giving waters.

In parts of North India, winter's chill can be uncomfortable, especially on January nights, but by February and early March, days and nights are extremely pleasant. Then the heat begins to build. In April and May—months that Westerners associate with balmy spring–much of India feels the harsh fist of desiccating heat. As temperatures soar well above 100 degrees F (ll5 degrees F in Rajasthan), swirling winds pick up dust from parched fields, and scorched travelers at train stations seek relief beneath ceiling fans in rooms specially reserved for cases of heat prostration. In cities, towns, and villages, all eagerly look forward to the monsoons.

Oftentimes the rains come in mid–June, or early July, when expected, and last until mid–September. Too frequently they are delayed, and sometimes, dreadfully, they fail. When the monsoons do come, tell-tale dark clouds announce their arrival. Suddenly, amid thunder and lightning, sheets of water cascade from the sky, soaking the thirsty fields and forests, inspiring the people to sing and dance with delight. It can rain for a week or more at a time, endless torrents from above ensuring that the crops will grow and the rivers flow for yet another year.

India has long been blessed with a richness of wildlife. Its forests and wetlands, dunes and grassy fields support an abundance of animals, ranging from magnificent carnivores to delicate butterflies. India's majestic national animal, the tiger, still stalks several protected regions, and the unique Indian lion roars in the Gir Forest in the western part of the country. Wild elephants roam free in limited regions of the far north and south, while large numbers of their domesticated cousins live all over the country. Panthers, wild bison, the one–horned rhinoceros, crocodiles, snakes, bears, storks, parrots, mischievous monkeys, and glorious peacocks are all part of the Indian scene. At dawn, in most of the country's many wildlife preserves, sun–dappled herds of spotted deer, antelope, and gazelle come out to graze on tawny grass wet with dew, reenacting a peaceful pageant of timeless beauty.

Irrevocably shaped by physical geography, ecology, and climate, each region of India has developed its own set of subcultures, expressing the people's response to the special conditions of each locale, unique, yet at the same time bound into the vast unity of the pan–Indian tradition.

Ancient Roots

The roots of Indian culture stretch back in time for untold hundreds of thousands of years. Archaeologists have found stone tools ranging from very early, crude hand axes to delicately chipped cutting implements, clues to the lifeways of hunters and gatherers who inhabited India's rich land. Sustained by wild plants and game, these wanderers moved seasonally from place to place, leaving behind in rock shelters colorful paintings of hunters, shamans, and animals. Even today, peoples of forest–dwelling tribes ornament their house walls with designs similar to the ancient cave paintings of millennia ago.

Gradually, India's prehistoric peoples began to keep cattle and grow crops, settling in villages, where they produced ceramic and metal objects. Reverence for cattle may have begun in these early times, perhaps four thousand years ago or more.

In the northwest of the Indian region–in the Indus River Valley, much of which is in Pakistan today–the growth of village culture was especially intense. In a dramatic burst of energy, the people of that region developed one of the earliest and greatest of the world's high cultures–the Indus Valley Civilization (also known as the Harappan Civilization). During the hundreds of years this civilization flourished, from 2500 B.C. to about 1600 B.C., the foundations of Hinduism and Indian culture were laid.

The remains of cities, with imposing buildings, paved streets, drains, shops, and homes, have all been uncovered by the archaeologist's spade, with even more constantly being revealed by researchers today. Fine wheel–turned pottery, ceramic figurines, and carved stone embossing seals have emerged from the Indus sites of Mohenjo–Daro, Harappa, and hundreds of others stretching over a territory more than a thousand miles long.

The carved stone seals are especially intriguing. Most are quite small, but they are exquisitely carved with figures of elephants, tigers, antelopes, and bulls, as well as with mysterious inscriptions that have yet to be definitively deciphered. The most famous seal depicts a horned godlike figure, sitting cross–legged, possibly an early version of Lord Shiva, one of modern Hinduism's greatest gods. Many scholars feel that the language of the seals and of the Indus Civilization was of the Dravidian family; Dravidian tongues are spoken by the

A young elephant enjoys his morning bath at Corbett National Park in northern India. Elephants are revered throughout the subcontinent.

Ancient paintings in a rock shelter in Madhya Pradesh, central India, provide glimpses of life as it was thousands of years ago. Today, some tribal peoples still ornament their homes with similar figures.

The Indus River gave life to India's earliest great civilization more than four thousand years ago. Here, near its source in the Himalayas, the Indus meets the Zanskar River.

majority of South Indians today.

As the Indus Civilization waned, it may have been hit with an enormous challenge–one of history's most important series of invasions–surges of Aryan–speaking nomads from Central Asia, who rode into India's northwest plains beginning about 1500 B.C. Thundering in on horses, the invaders cut a wide swath through the settled villages, apparently hastening the downfall of the peaceful civilization. The Aryan–speakers' warlike culture and nomadic predations changed India forever.

Attacking and conquering, and finally, mixing with the native Indian population, the Aryan–speakers became an essential part of their new land. Their Indo–Aryan language (related to the languages of Europe) gave rise to several North Indian languages, including ancient Sanskrit and modern Hindi, India's official national tongue. Their gods mingled with the Indus deities to become part of the Hindu pantheon, and their great books, the Vedas, have been revered in India for 3,500 years.

The four Vedic books, written in an old form of Sanskrit called Vedic, consist of hymns, prayers, and ritual instructions revealing much about religion and society during the thousand years of the Vedic Age, from about 1500 B.C. to 500 B.C. The rite of fire sacrifice lay at the heart of Vedic religion; fire sacrifice remains crucial in Hinduism today. And the rudiments of a system of categorizing people by birth and by occupation were laid down, echoed later in the elaborate caste system of medieval and modern India.

During the Vedic Age, settled villages grew up throughout much of peninsular India. As the Vedic Age progressed, iron technology–including iron plow shares, axes, and sickles–was introduced, thus opening vast areas of previously forested land to agriculture. These developments led to the growth of cities on the Gangetic plain–and to the dawn of Indian history.

The Flowering of Historic Culture

The sixth century B.C. was a time of rich cultural development and ferment in India. Trade and agriculture were thriving, and cities and kingdoms were growing. Philosophers were deeply engrossed in pondering the meaning of existence and human ties to the divine. Thinkers developed the concept of a single, all–encompassing spirit pervading the universe and manifested in all gods, all people, and all things. Other key ideas developed in these ancient days were the notion of a cycle of rebirth, or reincarnation; karma, or a destiny based on one's deeds in this life; and dharma, religious duty. These concepts remain central to Hinduism today.

The most famous Indian who ever lived was born about 567 B.C. in the foothills of the Himalayas. Siddhartha Gautama was a privileged prince who had access to forty thousand dancing girls, three palaces, and a beautiful wife and child. Destined to preach a new faith, he left his luxurious life behind and went forth as a mendicant, meditating upon eternal truths. Today we know him as the Buddha, the Enlightened One, founder of Buddhism, a faith born in India and promulgated throughout many lands of South, Southeast, and East Asia.

In about 520 B.C., another wealthy noble, Vardhamana, renounced the material world and become an ascetic mendicant. Honored today as he was twenty–five hundred years ago, he is known as Mahavira, the founder of Jainism, a religion that preaches strict nonviolence.

Other rulers were far less concerned with matters of the spirit and kept themselves busy with military conquests. In 531 B.C., Cyrus the Great of Persia led an invading army into northwest India, and for two centuries the Persians ruled the area with an iron hand. Then, in 331 B.C., Alexander the Great, the famous conquering Greek, led his troops in victory over the Persians. Within two years, Alexander had gone, but not without leaving important Greek influences behind. Next came Chandragupta Maurya, a North Indian who built India's first great empire, the Mauryan Empire, including almost all of India.

The Mauryan Empire was run with an effective system of military control, and the smallest signs of revolt were suppressed. The emperor led a life of great pomp and splendor. He wore fine robes embroidered in purple and gold and was borne forth on a gold litter lavishly ornamented with pearls. His attendants rode elephants encrusted with gold and silver. The emperor, however, did work to benefit his people.

Chandragupta's grandson Ashoka brought the Mauryan Empire to its height. He has been described by eminent historian A.L. Basham as "the greatest and noblest ruler India has known, and indeed one of the great kings of the world." Ashoka's edicts were carved in stone from the north to the south of India, testimony even today of the emperor's concern for his subjects. Ashoka led great battles, but then was horrified by the evils of war and converted to the nonviolent Buddhist faith. He renounced war and taught that people should treat others as they themselves wished to be treated. The lion motif, which adorned pillars of Ashoka's day, is the national emblem of modern India.

More invasions from Persia, Afghanistan, and Greek–influenced Central Asia followed. Few of these early invaders penetrated South India, which retained its special culture and developed its own independent kingdoms.

Hundreds of years later, in the fourth and fifth centuries, another great empire, the Gupta Empire, ruled North India. Famous for peace and prosperity, the age of the Guptas was a time of magnificent flowering of Hindu culture. Graceful sculptures of deities remain to remind us of the glories of the Guptas.

A confused period of invasions, dynasties, military attacks, and kingdoms followed. Eventually, a group of noble warriors, the Rajputs, came to dominate Indian history from about the ninth to the thirteenth centuries. Their code of chivalry resembled that of medieval Europe, with its respect for women and honorable conduct of war. Their stalwart forts and lavish Hindu temples were impressive, their courtly life elegant. Descendants of these warrior Rajputs are justly proud of their noble heritage.

The wealth of India continued to attract foreign invaders, and new waves of attackers swept across the subcontinent. These were the followers of Muhammad—Muslims from Arabia, Turkey, and Afghanistan–who came in successive onslaughts between the eighth and sixteenth centuries. While other invaders had been integrated into a tolerant and evolving Hinduism, the Muslims brought their own strong cultural and religious convictions. As the Muslims and Hindus clashed and ultimately settled down together, new facets were cut on the brilliant diamond of Indian civilization.

A chariot is driven in a royal procession through the streets of an ancient Indian city in this two–thousand–year–old relief at Sanchi, a Buddhist monument in central India.

A sari–draped woman peers from a latticed palace window at Amer, as generations of women did for centuries. A feature of many fine Indian structures, stone traceries admit light and air yet preserve privacy and cool temperatures.

The Magnificent Mughals

Muslim warriors, cultured Islamic scholars, as well as adventurers and fortune–seekers streamed into North India, establishing political and economic power over large areas. Even South India felt the sting of invasion, and there the great kingdom of Vijayanagar stood as a Hindu bulwark against Islam for 250 years.

Then in 1526, from Central Asia, came Babur—a descendant of the fierce Mongol Genghis Khan–who led his armies in conquest of most of the Gangetic plain. Babur became the first emperor of the splendid Mughal Empire, which would dominate India for three centuries. (Mughal is a corruption of the word Mongol.) Babur's descendants spread Mughal rule throughout the subcontinent, except for the southern tip.

The greatest Mughal emperor was Akbar, whose very name means "great." He exerted dominion over the Rajputs not only through military conquest, but by making them allies. Some of Akbar's several wives were Rajput princesses. He proclaimed tolerance for Hinduism, and even began a new religion integrating elements of Islam, Hinduism, Christianity, and other faiths. In this he showed himself to be like other great Indians of the past, seeking not only temporal power but an understanding of religious truths.

Akbar's son, Emperor Jahangir, brought Persian cultural influences into India, forever altering upper–class Indian manners and mores, as well as enriching language, literature, and the arts. The pride of Persianized Indo–Islamic architecture was created when Akbar's grandson, Emperor Shah Jahan, lost his beloved wife in 1631. Her memory is forever immortalized in the magnificent marble of the Taj Mahal.

While Hinduism and Islam gave much to each other, and a small proportion of Indians converted to the faith of the Prophet, the vast majority of Indians remained faithful Hindus. The great Hindu epic, the Ramayana, the story of the Hindu god Rama (also called Ram), achieved tremendous popularity during the Mughal period.

In fact, most subjects of the empire deeply resented the policies of Emperor Aurangzeb, a sternly orthodox Muslim who swept aside the tolerant measures of Akbar, his grandfather. Aurangzeb's hated repression of the Hindus ultimately contributed to the fatal weakening of the empire.

Rulers From Across the Sea

As their empire collapsed, challenged by Rajputs, by brave Maratha warriors from the Deccan, and then by marauders from Persia, the Mughals at first paid little heed to the growing number of Europeans drawn to India. In 1498, traveling by sea, lured by profits to be made in spices, jewels, and fabrics, the Portuguese arrived and later established trading posts along the western coast. In the early

The Mughal city of Fatehpur Sikri is adorned with structures rich in Hindu as well as Islamic elements. The city was occupied for a short time at the height of Mughal power.

In the shade of pink blossoms, Mughal arches grace the courtyard of the Taj Mahal in Agra. The rise of the Mughal Empire brought many changes to Indian society and culture.

seventeenth century, British traders landed. Dutch and French rivals also dropped anchor in Indian harbors.

Originally humble petitioners for trading rights at the opulent Mughal court, the British gradually expanded their ambitions to include rule of the whole of India. These unassuming merchants established Britain's East India Company, which would within two centuries replace the crumbling Mughal Empire with the British Raj.

Historic opportunity, greed, and skill combined to bring the British to power in India, which, at that time, included the areas of present–day Pakistan and Bangladesh. By 1765 the East India Company was exploiting much of the land, especially the rich region of Bengal, extracting goods and revenues from the gentle populace. Trade in indigo, cottons, and silk was burgeoning, and huge profits were being amassed. Finally tiring of the Company's abuses, Britain's Parliament declared its sovereignty over its dominions. By 1818, Britain held power over a huge proportion of India.

Resistance by Indian warriors and rajas was crushed, evaded, or carefully controlled. Dotting the territory directly ruled by the British were some 650 states ruled by Hindu and Muslim rulers, all recognized by the British.

Resentment of the foreign rulers exploded in 1857, in what has been called the Mutiny, the Sepoy Mutiny, or the First War for Indian Independence, when huge numbers of Indians arose to drive the English out. The Rani of Jhansi, the queen of a northern Indian state, rode to battle against the foreigners, and died in the saddle, a martyr in the cause of Indian independence. Some other rulers, however, knowing where the advantage lay, supported the British, and eventually the rebellion was subdued. In 1858 Queen Victoria proclaimed herself Empress of India. Fabulous profits and sumptuous goods continued to roll into Britain from India, the brightest gem in the crown of the British Empire.

Once again, the clash and mingling of cultures would change India forever, reshaping the ancient land into a new nation. Policies favoring British economic interests left some indigenous Indian institutions in shambles. British cloth goods flooded the Indian market, driving Indian weavers away from their centuries' old craft. Time–honored philosophies were challenged by unbelievers and by new ways of thinking from the West.

Perhaps without intending to ben-

The memory of British rule is still strong in India. At Calcutta's Victoria Memorial, the Queen–Empress remains regally enthroned.

efit India, the British did so in their introduction of the British Civil Service system—an administrative structure vital to India today. The railroad—some fifty thousand miles of steel rail, imported from British mills and paid for by Indians—has been essential to India's economic growth and development, as well as national unity. The British–style postal and telegraph services have also helped to tie the country together. Modern India's powerful army is organized along lines laid down by the British.

The use of the English language and English–style education also brought important change to India. English–speaking Indians could now communicate easily across this vast, multilingual land—and they could discuss ideas of independence and democracy, stimulated by sharing ideas with Western writers and thinkers.

Moving Toward Self–Rule

In 1893 a young Indian lawyer who had been trained in England went to South Africa to work in the Indian community there. He bought a ticket for a first–class train carriage—and was violently thrown out because of his skin color. Little did those who threw him out of the train car suspect that their act of raw bigotry would transform the shy barrister into an activist who would shake the very foundations of the British empire. The barrister was Mohandas K. Gandhi. Returning to his native land, he would become the spiritual father of Indian independence.

Inspired by both Hindu and Christian concepts of love and nonviolence, Gandhi argued that truth and love could move the world. He gave up his pin–striped suits and wrapped himself in the dhoti, the traditional Indian man's garment. A brilliant strategist very much in tune with the Indian populace—mostly villagers and working people—he praised ancient Indian values of simplicity. Gandhi preached against the evils of urban, industrialized society and foreign domination. His symbol of moral purity and self–reliance was a simple spinning wheel.

India's luxurious silks, like this gold–embroidered fabric from Bhopal, were among the attractions luring foreign traders, colonizers, and rulers to the subcontinent.

Revered by the masses, who called him Mahatma (Great Soul) and Bapu (Father), Gandhi urged Hindus and Muslims to love one another, high–status Hindus to treat low–status Untouchables with kindness and equality, and women to move out of seclusion into full participation in public life. Dramatically, he appealed to the British to leave India—and to help them along, organized and inspired nonviolent resistance all over the country.

With Gandhi as spiritual leader, more worldly politicians worked for decades in the halls of power to end British rule. Key leaders of the Indian National Congress were the urbane Motilal Nehru and his erudite son, Jawaharlal Nehru. Heading the militantly separatist Muslim League was the brilliant Mohammed Ali Jinnah.

Complex demands by all sides, along with the forces unleashed by World War II, finally led to the departure of the British from the subcontinent in 1947. From the ancient land of India two new nations were created—India and Muslim–dominated Pakistan. (Later, in 1971, Pakistan itself divided, when its eastern wing became the separate nation of Bangladesh.) The political partition of the land led to a traumatic movement of people and violence of every sort. Gandhi's dreams of peace were shattered. In January 1948, a Hindu fanatic assassinated the saintly leader, whose last words were "Hai Ram"—"Oh God."

Independent India's first prime minister was Jawaharlal Nehru, while Jinnah headed Pakistan. Nehru found himself leader of the world's largest democracy, a nation born in conflict yet committed to the highest ideals of religious freedom, equality, and justice. On the eve of independence, Nehru spoke dramatic words:

Long years ago we made a tryst with destiny and now the time comes when we shall redeem our pledge. ... A moment comes, which comes but rarely in history, when we step out from the old to the new, when an age ends and when the soul of a nation, long suppressed, finds utterance. It is fitting that at this solemn moment we take the pledge of dedication to the service of India and her people and to the still larger cause of humanity.

Since these noble words were spoken, dedicated leaders and hard–working citizens have striven to live up to these exalted ideals. The nation's course has not been a smooth one, yet the highest principles have guided India's progress as it has taken its place among the great civilizations of the modern world.

Honored throughout the nation as the father of independent India, Mohandas K. Gandhi advocated nonviolence as the means to move his country toward a hopeful future.

DEDICATION

THIS BOOK IS DEDICATED TO THE PEOPLE OF INDIA,
WHO MADE IT ALL POSSIBLE.

ACKNOWLEDGMENTS

I would like to express my deep appreciation to the many
people who have helped me to appreciate the complexity of
India's culture and civilization. Among those who have been
particularly helpful in the preparation of this volume are Dr.
Jerome Jacobson, Dr. Owen Lynch, Dr. Suzanne Hanchett,
Dr. John Walthall, Miss Sunalini Nayudu, Mr. Mirza Majid
Hussein Khan, Mrs. Rabiya Sultan Khan, Mr. Roy Moyer, and
Dr. Karl Lunde. I would like to thank these people as well as
Mr. Robert Tod and the photographers whose excellent work
has added so greatly to the beauty of this book.

*This book was designed and produced by
Todtri Productions Ltd*
P.O. Box 572
New York, NY 10116-0572
Fax: (212) 695-6988

Printed and bound in Korea

ISBN 1–880908–06–9

Author: Doranne Jacobson

Publisher: Robert Tod
Designer and Art Director: Mark Weinberg
Editor: Mary Forsell

TODTRI

Doranne Jacobson

INDIA
Land of Dreams and Fantasy

The Life of the Spirit

"In religion, all other countries are paupers. India is the only millionaire." So wrote Mark Twain on his visit to India in the late nineteenth century. Many more recent travelers have noted the wealth of religion and spirituality evident throughout the country. Everywhere, at all times, people in India are engaged in interaction with the divine, seeking to make things better in this life—or in the next.

There is a great diversity of religious traditions. Hindus, Muslims, Sikhs, Christians, Buddhists, Jains, Jews, Parsis, and Animists each worship in their own way. A multitude of shrines, temples, mosques, and churches ornament rural and urban landscapes, and brilliantly colorful religious rites and festivals enliven daily life.

Hinduism: A Tolerant Faith

Quietly, in the dim light of evening, a woman lights a tiny oil lamp and sets it on a shining brass platter beside fresh marigold blossoms and small portions of cooked food. She stands before a small altar in her home, where images of Lord Shiva, Goddess Parvati, Lord Ganesh, and other deities are displayed. Softly whispering prayers, she slowly rotates the glowing platter before the gods, honoring them and expressing her hopes that they will help protect her and her family.

Drums beat and cymbals clash as musicians lead the way for a dazzlingly decorated elephant bearing on its back a silver throne and a bearded holy man. Leader of a monastery, the holy man is surrounded by his ocher–robed followers, progressing slowly through an immense crowd of millions of people. All are moving across the sands to the hallowed confluence of three sacred rivers—the Ganga, the Jamna, and the mythic Saraswati—where they will bathe at an auspicious moment in astrological time. At the best–attended event on earth, as far as the eye can see, masses of pilgrims are moving, singing, praying, all striving toward the same goal—ritual cleansing in waters sacred for thousands of years.

Hinduism takes many forms, from serene private prayer to cacophonous public festival. Hindus say there are 330 million gods and goddesses–and yet all are manifestation of One. Some worship Lord Shiva with special ardor, while others prefer Vishnu. Krishna, Ganesh, Jagannath, Durga, Ram, Gauri, Lakshmi, and Bemata are other favorite deities, and there are thousands more. Each village, each family, each clan has a protective deity, and there are countless spirits and ghosts guarding crossroads and dwellings. Some deities prefer strictly vegetarian offerings, while others are satisfied only with a blood sacrifice. To ignore the needs and wishes of divine beings is to court disaster, for only with their help can humans achieve prosperity.

The modern Lakshmi Narayan Temple in New Delhi was built by the Birlas, a prosperous family of industrialists. The colorful Hindu complex is dedicated to Vishnu (Narayan) and his wife Lakshmi, the Goddess of Wealth.

Sunrise lights the sacred Ganges— or Ganga—River, at the holy city of Varanasi, as a devout Hindu worshipper pours holy water on a lingam, symbolic of Lord Shiva.

Lakshmi, the Hindu Goddess of Wealth, is surrounded by auspicious figures in this modern print found in many homes. Saraswati, the Goddess of Learning, is seated at left, while Ganesh, the elephant–headed God of Good Fortune, is on the right.

Hymns of praise for Lord Krishna and his consort, Radha, are sung daily at a prosperous Hindu home in Bombay, where the deity is enshrined in a family chapel. Fresh flowers adorn the sacred images and altar.

Lord Krishna, the playful flute-playing god beloved of millions of Hindus, is portrayed in a children's pageant at a religious fair at Pushkar, Rajasthan. The god is attended by faithful female devotees.

Hinduism is the most tolerant of religions, for it accepts into its fold almost any deity and any form of worship. Many philosophical views and concepts of the divine are embraced within Hinduism, and there is no dogma, no single religious leader to say that any version of worship is wrong. The religion has evolved over so long a time, and included so many peoples and their supernatural protectors, that it is a rich multiplicity of approaches to God.

Two ancient texts have been close to Hindu hearts for some two thousand years. The Mahabharata, or the Great Epic, describes a heroic war, discusses key philosophies, and includes the Bhagavad Gita—or the Song of God—the most luminous of all Hindu scriptures. The Ramayana tells the story of the God–King Rama and his devoted wife, Sita. These epics reinforce prized Hindu values.

Hindu rituals tend to be colorful and almost sensuous, involving offerings of flowers, leaves, fruits, spicy foods, sweets, coconuts, water, milk, golden turmeric paste, and even silver, gold, and precious gems. The invisible deities are represented by a wonderful complexity of images, many with multiple arms symbolizing their divine powers, all holding signs of their special potencies. Through their rituals, Hindus interact closely with the divine. Seeing the divine images is important; the gods, in return, gaze upon their mortal worshippers, revealing their regard and concern. Many of these sacred images are housed within ornate temples of unsurpassed beauty.

More than four–fifths of Indians are Hindus (eighty–three percent), and their religion is an integral part of virtually every aspect of life. Hinduism, and one's place within it, affects social status, diet, work, family life, concepts of duty, and expectations for the future. Dharma, righteous conduct, karma, the fruits of one's deeds, and moksha, liberation from the cycle of death and rebirth, are concerns that virtually all Hindus share.

Life's passages—birth, religious initiation, marriage, and death—are marked with elaborate ceremonies invoking the influences of the cosmos. Weddings can be especially spectacular events. The progress of the Hindu year is plotted according to the sacred lunar–solar calendar and celebrated in a gorgeous array of festivals—some pan–Indian, others more regional. For sheer delight, nothing can match the exuberant joy of Hindu festival celebrations.

To see divine images and to experience personal contact with Mother India's sacred landscape, Hindus travel on pilgrimages to holy rivers, mountains, oceans, and temples at all corners of the country. Pilgrims tread the very ground where the infant Lord Krishna played; they journey to view the holy peaks where the Gods live; they immerse themselves in the liquid sanctity of the Goddess Ganga; and they travel to Rameshwaram, on the southern tip of the subcontinent, to take darshan—a holy viewing—of the very symbol of Shiva that Lord Ram established after rescuing his wife, Sita, from her evil kidnapper. For Hindus today, deities and mythology are very much alive, and pilgrimage is as important as it was for Christians at the height of the Middle Ages in Europe. Through their reverent travels, Hindu pilgrims enhance their knowledge of their country and knit together their vast community of hundreds of millions of worshippers.

The delicate towers and turrets of the red sandstone Moti Masjid (Pearl Mosque) ornament Bhopal's sunset skyline.

Islam: The Faith of the Prophet

"There is but one God, Allah, and Muhammad is his Prophet." This simple declaration states the essence of Islam, the great religion born in Arabia in the seventh century and spread throughout much of the world. God's revelations to Muhammad are preserved in Arabic in the Holy Koran, the sacred book all Muslims revere.

With nearly 100 million adherents to the faith, (some 11.5 percent of the population) India has one of the largest Muslim populations in the world. Like Muslims everywhere, most attempt to follow the precepts of Islam—prayer five times daily, facing Mecca, where Islam was founded in A.D. 622, giving alms to the poor, fasting during the

symbol of fertility for a Hindu bride, has its counterpart in turmeric unguents applied to Muslim brides. Why not? Although Islamic laws are precise on many points, there is much room for emotionally fulfilling variation.

Muslim mystics and saints have sought to know God in ways that Hindu holy men would understand. The tombs of many Indian Muslim saints have become shrines where Muslims in need of succor can come to pray, even as Hindu shrines provide the same focus for Hindu devotees. Some tombs and shrine attract both Hindu and Muslim supplicants.

Hindus and Muslims sometimes provoke one another, but in every village, town, and city, Hindus and Muslims have lived side by side for centuries, their temples and mosques bearing tangible witness to the cultural wealth they have shared with each other.

month of Ramadan from sunup to sundown, and, if possible, making the great pilgrimage to Mecca, the geographic center of Islamic devotion.

A thousand years of interacting with Hinduism, and recruiting most of its adherents from among Hindu ranks, has given Indian Islam its own special flavor. Although fewer in number and somewhat more austere than Hindu festivals, Islamic holidays are embellished with a special brilliance that is uniquely Indian. Muslim kinship and weddings, while different from Hindu practices in important respects, reflect the complexity and love of life so characteristic of India. For one small example, golden turmeric ointment, an essential

"God is great," proclaims a Muslim worshipper facing toward Mecca as he kneels in evening prayer. About one—eighth of Indians are followers of the Islamic faith.

Sikhism: Inspiration of the Divine Teacher

The Sikh faith was founded by Guru Nanak (1469–1539), inspired by the devotional Hinduism of his family and by mystical Islam. "There is no Hindu, there is no Muslim. There is only One Being Who is the Creator ... God is One," he declared. Deeply spiritual, Guru Nanak preached goodness and tolerance across North India, welcoming all to his new religion.

For Sikhs, their holy book, Guru Granth Sahib, is the object of their highest veneration. No graven images adorn their temples, the most famous of which is the Golden Temple in Amritsar, Punjab, with its walls and dome covered with pure gold.

As Mughal rulers, and later the British, challenged the Sikh faithful, they became increasingly militant in defense of their religious community. Recent conflict between Sikhs and India's government leaders in New Delhi has deep historic roots going back centuries.

Today, some seventeen million strong, most Sikhs bear the surname Singh—Lion—symbolizing their militant determination. As signs of their faith, traditional Sikh men keep their hair and beard uncut, bind their hair up with a small comb and a distinctive turban, wear undershorts so that they may always be ready for battle, wear a steel bracelet, and keep a sword or dagger on their person. Thus distinguished, followers of the line of divine teachers initiated by Guru Nanak are recognizable anywhere in the world, their faith inspiring them with a special energy.

Buddhism and Jainism: Creeds of Nonviolence

The creed of nonviolence preached by Lord Buddha flourished in ancient India. More than two thousand years ago, adherents of this deeply philosophical faith turned away from eating meat and from sacrificing animals to the deities. They also rejected strict rules of caste that had grown up in Indian society. Over the centuries, Buddhism gained many converts in distant lands but almost died out in the land of its birth.

In India today, Buddhists dwell in the northernmost fringes of the country, particularly along the borders of Buddhist Tibet and Nepal. A newer group of converts to Buddhism is growing in the heart of western and northern India. These are members of groups formerly known as Untouchables, who reject the low position they have been allocated in Hindu society. Following their late honored leader, Dr. B.R. Ambedkar, who helped draft independent India's constitution, these new Buddhists number some five million. Their heartfelt practice of India's ancient faith of enlightenment has added a dimension of self–respect to their lives.

Jainism, too, grew up in ancient India and today inspires the devotions of a few million people. Jains see all life as sacred and all creatures as imbued with souls. Very strictly orthodox Jain monks and nuns wander northern India. They use a whisk to sweep the path before them as they walk, so they will not unwittingly commit the sin of killing an insect or an earthworm. To avoid ingesting even the smallest mite, they also wear a gauze mask over the mouth.

More worldly Jains are strict vegetarians and strain their drinking water through a fine cloth to protect tiny aquatic creatures from being consumed. Since even plowing the earth is considered likely to cause the deaths of small animals, Jains have followed nonagricultural pursuits, such as commerce and

Inside a Sikh house of worship, or gurudwara, in Maharashtra State, devotees honor their holy book and the spiritual teachers of their faith. Sikhs are a prominent minority throughout India.

A Buddhist image, brilliant with gold, is an object of great veneration at Thikse Monastery in the Ladakh region, high in the Himalayas.

Nuns of the Jain faith gather at a monk's initiation ceremony in Ahmedabad, Gujarat. Jain nuns usually wander from place to place in small groups, avoiding all worldly involvements and practicing complete nonviolence.

Christianity has ancient roots in Indian soil–St. Thomas is said to have brought the faith to India nearly two thousand years ago. This small church in Goa reflects the influence of the Portuguese, who arrived in 1498.

A tribal amulet from Bastar in central India depicts a bison–horned deity. The amulet is cast in brass by the lost–wax process.

banking, and have become one of the most prosperous communities in India.

Jain temples are often very well endowed and beautifully maintained. Exquisite carved marble statuary and brilliant mirrored murals provide radiant settings for devout prayer.

Faiths From Afar

By tradition, Christianity was brought to India by Christ's doubting apostle, St. Thomas, who landed on the Malabar coast nearly two thousand years ago. More recently, in 1544, St. Francis Xavier evangelized along the western coast of India, and his remains are enshrined in a cathedral in Goa. Since the British period, western missionaries have been active on the subcontinent. Today, more than twenty million Christians of every denomination practice their faith throughout India.

Jewish settlers arrived on the Malabar coast in A.D. 72, as part of the Diaspora. More Jews came in the fifteenth century, fleeing Spanish persecution. Middle Eastern Jews later added to the multiethnic Jewish mix. Many Indian Jews have left for Israel, but several thousand remain to worship in the synagogues of Bombay and Cochin.

Fire–worshipping Persians of the Zoroastrian faith fled Muslim intolerance in their own land in the eighth century and were welcomed by Hindu rulers of western India. They proved to be able merchants and founded some of India's great commercial enterprises. Parsis, as they are known, are prominent citizens of many cities, especially Bombay, where their sacred fires are tended in inconspicuous temples. To avoid polluting the sacred elements of fire and earth, Parsis dispose of their dead in Towers of Silence, where vultures clean the bodies of the deceased.

Tribal Faiths

Sprinkled throughout India are the descendants of some of the country's original inhabitants—people for whom the bearers of Indus Valley and Aryan culture were newly arrived upstarts. For these tribal peoples, local spirits and deities are very much alive in the trees and stones around them. Many elements of tribal religions have gradually been incorporated into Hinduism, and interaction between the local and the overarching traditions continues today.

The Social Order

India is well known as a land of almost limitless social complexity. India's people belong to large numbers of families, lineages, clans, castes, and religious and ethnic groups, as well as social and economic classes. Differences in education and access to wealth, land, and other resources are enormous. Despite these awesome complexities, Indian society is carefully ordered according to respected principles of kinship and other social and economic bonds. Within the numerous hierarchies of the society, each person has a place and a sense of secure identity.

Families are Foremost

The blare of bugles and the rhythm of drums resound through the mud–walled lanes of an Indian village. An exuberant wedding party is nearing the groom's home after several days of festivities at the bride's distant home. With the party is the shy and silent bride, swathed in drapery so that none of new in–laws can see her face. She is entering for the first time her husband's village and his home, where she will spend much of the rest of her life.

Guests and relatives crowd around to witness the greetings and blessings being bestowed upon the couple by members of the groom's joint family–the young man's grandparents, parents, brothers and their wives and children, and younger, unmarried sisters and brothers. The shy young bride is a welcome addition to the family, for she will join in household chores, lightening the burden for all. More importantly, she brings with her the possibility of adding treasured children to the household, helping ensure the family's continuance and prosperity.

Now embarrassed and insecure, married to a man selected by her parents and whom she has but barely glimpsed, the new bride will soon become acquainted with her husband. Over the years she may well become the mother of sons and daughters and will be a force to be reckoned with in the household. If fortune smiles on her and her husband, one day they too will stand in the doorway of their home to welcome their sons and their new brides.

Joint families and larger groups of relatives are the underpinnings of Indian society. For most Indians, the ideal household consists of three or four generations, all living under one roof, working, eating, worshipping, and laughing together. In most parts of India, joint families include men related through the male line, along with their wives and children. Most young women expect to live with their husband's relatives after marriage.

The joint family is an ancient Indian institution, but it has undergone some change in recent decades. Although the ideal is several generations living together, actual living arrangements vary widely with region, social status, and economic circumstance. Many Indians today live in so–called nuclear families—a couple with their unmarried children—like the most common pattern in the West. Sometimes clusters of

A Rajasthani couple and their daughter enjoy each other's company. Members of Indian families learn to depend on each other for support and lasting affection.

Surrounded by loving members of her family, a village bride in Madhya Pradesh is readied for her marriage. To help ensure her fertility, her skin is anointed with golden turmeric paste.

Hindu youths are invested with the sacred thread at an important rite of passage celebrated within the family circle. The boys belong to the high-ranking Jijotiya Brahman priestly caste.

Within a ritual shelter looped with fragrant jasmine garlands, a bride and groom in Coorg enjoy their first few moments of marriage. Relatives bless the well–educated couple with gestures of respect and light auspicious votive lamps. The styles of dress are unique to upland Coorg.

relatives live very near each other, always handy for getting together.

Large families are flexible and well suited to modern Indian life, especially for the majority of Indians who are farmers or farm workers. The joint family is also common in cities, where kinship ties can be crucial to getting scarce jobs or financial assistance. In fact, like the American Kennedys or Rockefellers, large Indian families, such as the Tatas, Birlas, and Sarabhais, control some of the country's most prominent financial empires.

As joint families grow ever larger, they inevitably divide into smaller units, carrying out a predictable cycle over time. Even when relatives do not actually live together, they usually feel strong bonds of kinship and provide each other with economic help, emotional support, and other benefits.

The values of joint family living stress group harmony. Individuals learn to shape their wills to the needs of the family and acceptance of the authority of older relatives. As in the rest of Indian life, hierarchy is important even within the home. In general, males command more authority than females, and elders more than younger family members.

For growing children, joint families bring special advantages. Children learn love and cherished values from grandparents, as well as from aunts and uncles, and they enjoy playing with cousins of all ages. Indian children learn to think of themselves not as autonomous individuals, but as parts of a group of caring kin. For elders, too, joint family living brings great joy, as they live surrounded by children and grandchildren. It is within the bosom of the family that each person passes through the phases of his or her life, each milestone marked by a rite or ceremony. At birth, a child's advent is hailed by drums and the distribution of sweets. At or before puberty, a young man might be invested with the Hindu sacred thread, looped over the left shoulder and across his upper body to remind him of his religious obligations. In South India, a young girl's maturity is often celebrated with special foods and gifts. At death, funeral observances bring kin groups together to remind each other of the importance of the departed and the continuing bonds that tie the living together.

But among life's passages, it is marriage that takes on the most ceremonial importance. In villages and in cities, most marriages are arranged by elders, and almost all young people happily abide by the choices made for them. As Indians are fond of saying, love usually comes after marriage, rather than before. However, among college–educated young people, so–called love marriages are becoming more common. Still, it is not unusual for a young man or woman completing an advanced professional degree to agree to an arranged marriage. Among Muslims and some South Indian Hindus, cousins may marry, and secret crushes sometimes result in joyful wedlock.

Weddings are a time to splurge–each family typically spending more than it can afford on a grand event uniting not just a couple but two large sets of kin. Weddings can indeed be ostentatious—for the well–to–do, colored lights, scarlet–uniformed musicians, a gold–spangled horse or a fancy car to convey the groom, costly silks and sumptuous gold jewelry for the bride, huge feasts of elaborately prepared foods for hundreds of guests, complex religious rituals, abundant garlands of fragrant flowers, and a host of lavish gifts and cash payments. Festivities often go on for days and remain in the memory as times of great significance.

Being closely involved with many relatives requires compromises, to be sure, but most of India's people take pleasure in the intense human feeling that is the essence of extended family life.

The Fellowship of Caste

Almost all of India's hundreds of millions of people are born into and marry within one of thousands of castes and castelike groups. The caste system developed over millennia, linking groups in a complex hierarchy. In essence, a caste is a group of people who claim a common origin and who marry among themselves. Traditionally, each caste has been associated with a rank and occupation. In each locale, caste members know which of their neighbors belong to higher–ranking groups and which to lower. Typically, a single village settlement includes members of many castes. Some castes have representatives in only a few villages, while the members of other castes are much more widespread. For virtually everyone in India, social hierarchy is a matter of everyday concern, shaping many aspects of personal and community life.

Caste–associated occupations range from high–ranking Brahmans (priestly castes) and middle–ranking farmers and merchant groups, to lower–ranking artisan groups, such as potters, weavers, barbers, and carpenters, and "untouchable" launderers, butchers, leatherworkers, and latrine–cleaners. Traditionally, caste has provided a framework for potential exploitation, yet, in general, members of different castes have been interdependent, cooperating in symbiotic systems of some benefit to all.

The greatest number of castes are found among the Hindus, but even Muslims, Christians, and Sikhs recognize caste differences among themselves. In fast–changing modern India, caste is taking on new meanings. "Untouchability" and negative discrimination have been outlawed, and some members of formerly low–status groups are attaining honored positions in the professions and politics. People of all castes are free to seek employment in the full range of available occupations. For some, contacts with caste–fellows can lead to employment. Caste membership can provide a sense of security in belonging to a large fellowship of people who care about each other.

A weaver practices his craft, creating fine shawls and blankets. Such specialized skills are often passed from one generation to another, within a single caste. The fellowship of caste is important to most Indians.

The Partnership of the Sexes

Swashbuckling men with jewel–studded daggers, silk–veiled women with tinkling bangles, valorous soldiers defending their forts and families, retiring maidens praying for their defenders' well–being: these are ideal stereotypical images of Indian men and women. While these roles are enacted to perfection by stars of the popular Indian cinema, real life calls for men and women to play a variety of other parts.

Everywhere in India, one is struck by the social differences between men and women, and the sense that neither can do without the other. The sexes constantly complement one another.

In this land of thousands of years of invasion and conquest, male dominance is almost a basic assumption. Ancient scriptures praise male supremacy over women, and even today, the birth of a son is almost always cause for greater celebration than the birth of a daughter. Most agricultural land, the basis of the economy, is owned by men.

Yet, in her time, Prime Minister Indira Gandhi was the world's most powerful woman, holding tight the reigns of government over hundreds of millions of people for fifteen years. All over the country, women work at a variety of tasks, making essential contributions to their families' survival, even as men do. Almost as if to acknowledge this, the Hindu pantheon is full of beautiful strong goddesses who control human life. Even the mighty Hindu gods are powerless without the special energy provided by their divine female consorts. In modern India, the feminist movement is growing.

Indian women are a study in contrasts. Many are adorned with vivid clothing and carry themselves with elegance as they go about their work, both at menial jobs and in the highest professions. Others are shabbily dressed, excessively burdened by their labors. Some confidently address classes and conferences, while a great number veil their faces and shrink from public view. Time–honored standards of female modesty are followed by the vast majority of rural women, while urban women tend to adopt newer modes of expressing their femininity.

Men, too, display a variety of images. Many are proudly virile, confident of their prestige, while others, less privileged, must adopt a lower profile. Still, a larger number of men than women appear at ease in public, working and socializing without shyness. Their dress is usually less brilliant than that of women, even as their conduct is more flamboyant.

Everyone in India thinks a great deal about the proper relations between the sexes, and ideals are displayed not only in films, but in temple art, literature, advertisements, and religious ceremonies. Ideally, a chaste woman is entitled to honor and respect, even as she upholds her family's honor by being true to her husband. In Hindu legend, the faithful wife Savitri literally saved her husband from the clutches of the God of Death through her chaste devotion. Thus, by gracefully seeming to accept a subordinate status, women control a unique power over the lives and prosperity of their families, even as men exert power through their more overtly dominant roles.

These ambiguities in the relationships between men and women are

Lord Shiva and his wife Parvati are depicted in eternal partnership in this popular print. Even a mighty deity like Shiva is considered powerless without the special energy provided by his female counterpart. Similarly, in the Indian view, men and women complement each other in daily life.

A Hindu holy man, wearing a topknot and long matted tresses like Lord Shiva, visits Shiva's holy city of Varanasi. He is an ascetic wanderer and has renounced family life to seek spiritual salvation.

played out in the complex conditions of everyday life. Men and women acknowledge in many ways their dependence on each other for creating and maintaining their families and their happiness.

The Fringes of Society

At every religious fair, crowded pilgrimage site, and worshipper–filled temple they appear, their faces gray with ashes and their hair long and matted. Some wear ocher robes and brilliant face paint. They are Hindu sadhus, or holy men, who have renounced normal family life and have pledged themselves to live as religious mendicants, wandering from one sacred place to another. An estimated five million men, and a few thousand women as well, have moved away from worldly responsibilities to seek enlightenment and ultimate union with the Universal Soul. Distinguished by their unusual dress—or lack of it (some go naked to announce their complete lack of concern with material goods), they live an ascetic life, undergoing physical privations to gain spiritual strength.

Some sadhus make a special effort to emulate Lord Shiva, with his long hair and body covered with ashes from cremation grounds. A few undertake remarkable vows—such as ceaselessly standing on one foot for twelve years, as Lord Shiva did. Devotees admire most sadhus' spirituality and provide them with food and shelter, but cynics believe some sadhus may be frauds.

India is full of ascetics, saints, and mystics. The most famous living saint, Satya Sai Baba, apparently performs miracles and is the favorite of well–educated devotees, to whom he brings a sense of cultural identity and fatherlike protection in a fast–changing world. Many other mystics, less well known, manipulate spirits and ghosts to cure disturbed patients. Their success rate is high.

Other unique people to be encountered on India's byways include the hijras, or eunuchs, men who wear women's dress. They come from a variety of unhappy situations but find joy in their new identity, protected by their own Hindu goddess. Groups of eunuchs are often invited to sing and dance in celebration at homes where baby boys have been born.

The Village Community

More than three–quarters of India's population lives in villages. Some half–million villages dot the map, ranging from tiny hamlets of thatched huts to larger settlements of stone houses with tile roofs. The essential business of village India is agriculture–the production of food for nearly 900 million people. India is self–sufficient in agricultural production.

Farmers follow time–tested methods of growing wheat, rice, lentils, vegetables, fruits, and myriad other crops, knowing that there is little scope in their budgets to allow for costly mistakes. Bullock–drawn plows are the implement of choice for most farmers, but some have been able to afford petrol–hungry tractors. The Green Revolution and new drilled wells have brought more abundant crops to some regions, but with these have come greater dependence on chemical fertilizers and erratic supplies of electricity and gasoline. Indian farmers are forever challenged by the magnitude of their task: using a piece of land and a plow to produce food and sustenance for their families–and for the nation.

Indian villagers work at a wide array of tasks, with men and women busy from before dawn till after sundown. Men plow and thresh the grain, while women join in sowing, transplanting, weeding, harvesting, and winnowing. Women take charge of food processing and cooking, preparing delicious meals over modest earthen stoves. Dried cow dung cakes and ever–scarcer wood fuel village kitchens.

Cattle have a very special place in the lives of villagers. Cows, bullocks, and water buffaloes are all extremely useful animals. Cows and buffaloes give milk, important to nutrition. Cows also give birth to bullocks, essential as draft animals who pull the plows through the thick, damp earth. Without bullocks, no crops could be grown. And all of these bovines eat straw and otherwise useless vegetation, converting it to dung, vital as both fertilizer and fuel. Such valuable animals are given names and are well cared for. Hindu ideals forbid the

In the golden light of evening, an ox–drawn cart laden with sheaves of grain heads for home. The harvests reaped by India's villagers feed the huge nation.

slaughter of cattle. In some areas, goats, camels, and even elephants are valuable domestic animals.

Village artisans keep ancient crafts alive. Women plaster and paint their homes in traditional designs, and some embroider ornate items to wear or display. Village potters shape terra–cotta water pots and figurines, even as Harappan potters did thousands of years ago. Weavers, cloth dyers, carpenters, and metal workers all create objects of remarkable beauty, incorporating patterns of great antiquity. Some village men still wear traditional turbans and wrap–around garments, and most village women dress in regional costumes ornamented with intricate jewelry. Perhaps no place else on earth nurtures as wide a variety of living folk art traditions as does India today.

Treasured cultural forms also flourish in the villages. Devout worship at local shrines, colorful festival celebrations, traditional wedding observances, folk dances and dramas, and old–fashioned family values are all part of village life.

The joy of the harvest and of the unity of the village community is celebrated at the Holi festival in India's heartland. Village men dance, sing, and splatter each other with dye to express their delight.

Decorated with painted designs and ornaments, a village bullock is pampered on the Hindu festival of Divali. Cattle are honored for the essential role they play in the village economy.

The Growing Cities

While some would locate India's cultural heart in its villages, many see the cities as the wave of the future. Villagers and townsfolk seeking opportunities are migrating to the cities in record numbers. The country's dozen largest cities—Calcutta, Bombay, Delhi, Madras, Hyderabad, Ahmedabad, Bangalore, Kanpur, Pune, Nagpur, Lucknow, and Jaipur—together represent every segment of the nation. Commerce and industry are growing apace—India is, after all, the tenth largest industrial nation in the world.

Cities offer crowded living conditions—and job opportunities, educational options, well–supplied markets, packed cinema houses, and a throbbing vitality that can only be engendered when millions of people are working and playing in close proximity to one another.

Indian city streets are incredibly busy, with sometimes cacophonous traffic, noisy hawkers, surging crowds, and rushing entrepreneurs of every sort. There is no idleness—everyone has a job to do and must be quick about it. Making a living is seldom easy.

Cultural life includes not only the folk observances that people have brought from the villages, but also traditional urban practices and modern innovations. Classical Indian dances and ancient Sanskrit dramas are performed in concert halls not far from galleries of modern art, cricket fields, and the studios of avant–garde architects. Parades honoring ancient deities proceed past sparkling new office buildings and luxury hotels. Life in an Indian city is indeed stimulating, uniting the old and the new with a matchless vibrancy.

India's cities are growing fast, as many rural folk move to urban areas to seek their fortunes. Here, Bombay's Marine Drive (now Netaji Subhash Road) throbs with energy.

Cultural life in urban India is full of variety. This woman performs classical dances of great antiquity before appreciative city audiences.

From Past to Future

Since the nation achieved independence in 1947, India has made huge strides. Dramatic progress has been made in agricultural production, industrial expansion, education, health care, communications, human rights, social services, and in many other realms. Indian mathematicians and scientists are recognized the world over for their ground–breaking accomplishments. India–trained physicians staff fine health facilities not only in India but in many other countries. Mortality rates have fallen, while literacy rates have risen. Institutions of higher learning are full of eager students. Steel mills, atomic energy plants, heavy electrical facilities, and many other technologically advanced industries have sprung up on Indian soil. Electricity has reached a high proportion of villages, and television sets have proliferated in the cities and in the countryside.

Like other developing nations, India faces many problems. Its population has grown two and a half times since independence. Social and economic inequities remain. Urban housing is scarce for people of modest means, and for many, unemployment is a major difficulty. In villages, health care and fair distribution of land are serious concerns.

As India moves into the future, it will draw upon its rich cultural heritage to help smooth the way. For thousands of years, Indian culture has absorbed influences from all over the world and integrated them into an ever more all–encompassing tradition, and modern challenges will surely be met in the same inspired way. The kaleidoscope of India's splendid civilization will continue to shine with beauty and brilliance.

Following page:
The Taj Mahal, the greatest of India's Mughal monuments, rises majestically behind men and camels in Agra, once capital of the mighty Mughal Empire.

The Historic North

The great Gangetic Plain of North India has proven to be fertile ground for the growth of Indian culture and the rise and fall of imperial powers. Everywhere, there are monuments to the past in the midst of the rapid pulses of modern life.

Delhi: Many Times a Capital

The Jama Masjid, one of India's largest mosques, holds thousands of worshippers on the Islamic feast day of Id. Shah Jahan worshipped here more than three centuries ago.

The capital of the world's largest democratic nation rings with political debate, in the halls of parliament, in the press, and in the streets. Delhi is the active political center of a lively nation—parades, demonstrations, and the ordinary hustle and bustle of government business are all around. Splendidly uniformed guards and military officers are a common sight.

Actually, Delhi is not a single city. There has been a series of seven royal capitals here, capped off by present–day Old Delhi and New Delhi, majestic halves of the modern metropolis most Indians call simply Delhi.

An ancient settlement, Indraprastha, on the banks of the Jamna River, has left archaeological remains dating to the third or fourth century B.C. Some believe this town was founded by the Pandava brothers, mythical heroes of the epic Mahabharata.

During medieval times, Hindu and then Muslim rulers built a grand sequence of structures to commemorate their power. All around the Delhi region stand the imposing remnants of walls, forts, arches, towers, palaces, and tombs, each bearing testimony to human effort and temporality. For the people of modern Delhi, while traveling to work or school, it is usual to pass structures built many centuries apart. Here history is part of everyday life.

A soaring tower of early Muslim victory, the Qutb Minar, attracts many visitors. Impressively ornate, its construction was begun in the twelfth century. Beautiful calligraphy adorns the adjacent edifices. But even these antique structures are young compared with the nearby fifth–century iron pillar dating from the Gupta period. The metal is of exceptional purity and has never rusted.

The Delhi Zoo is built near the site of Purana Qila, or Old Fort, dating from the mid-sixteenth century. Happy schoolchildren and cheerful families on outings gaze at caged tigers not far from the old sandstone tower where Mughal Emperor Humayan struck his head and died. Nearby is his tomb, a fine example of early Mughal architecture. The elements in its design—a short building graced by high–arched entrances and a pointed dome—were later refined and reshaped into the magnificence of Agra's Taj Mahal.

Of all of Delhi's time–worn monuments, those built during the reign of the Mughal Emperor Shah Jahan are the most impressive. Looming over the old city are the imposing crenelated russet sandstone

The Qutb Minar, a soaring tower dating from the twelfth century, commemorates a Muslim victory. Adjacent structures are ornamented with carved calligraphy.

The fine tomb of Mughal Emperor Humayan is adorned with pointed arches and decorative stonework. Elements of the tomb's design were preludes to the elegant architecture of the Taj Mahal.

walls of the Red Fort, Lal Qila. Within are the delicate white marble Pearl Mosque and the once–resplendent Hall of Private Audience, where the emperor sat in splendor upon the magnificent Peacock Throne. This masterpiece of fine gems and gold was carted off to Persia, along with an enormous amount of fabulous loot, by the plundering Nadir Shah in 1739. Today one finds only the inscription of a famous Persian couplet to invoke past glories:

If there is a paradise on earth
it is this, it is this, it is this.

In Shah Jahan's time, a tree–shaded avenue beautified by fountains and lovely shops laden with brocades, gems, ivory, and fine carpets led from the fort toward the great mosque, Jama Masjid. The avenue, Chandni Chauk—Moonlight Plaza—was crowded with a moving mosaic of the peoples of the Mughal Empire. Today it is still crowded, with a potpourri of trucks, motor rickshaws, oxcarts, motorcycles, pedestrians, and sidewalk vendors.

Shah Jahan's mosque still draws impressive throngs of worshippers, especially on the two annual Id holidays, when thousands prostrate themselves to the Almighty within the walled courtyard of the domed seventeenth–century structure.

On January 26 of every year, the world's greatest parade proceeds down Rajpath, New Delhi's grand royal avenue, from the imposing Secretariat buildings to the triumphal arch, India Gate. To celebrate Republic Day, folk dancers from every state, marching soldiers, uniformed students, cultural floats, gold–caparisoned elephants, tanks, and jet planes parade before a gigantic crowd of city folk and villagers.

This grandiose display of Indian national unity and accomplishment takes place in a setting designed to glorify British rule. The British had their viceregal capital at Calcutta, but in 1911 decided to move it to Delhi. Two architects, Edwin Lutyens and Herbert Baker, designed the new capital of British India, high-

Chandni Chauk–Moonlight Plaza–was Mughal Delhi's finest avenue. Today it is busy with traffic of every kind and ablaze with bright billboards advertising swashbuckling musical movies.

A Sikh merchant at Chandni Chauk sells steel bracelets, worn by all Sikh men as essential symbols of their militant faith. Many Sikhs live in Delhi.

New Delhi is vibrant with activity in government, commerce, and the arts. A modern artist stands before his painting of a South Indian seashore.

Outside the Red Fort, a snake charmer displays a python and a hooded cobra. Cobras and other venomous serpents can be quite dangerous, but this man has perfected his snake–handling skills from childhood.

Firmly gripping their rifles, women members of India's armed forces march in the Republic Day parade, providing a notable contrast to traditional feminine roles.

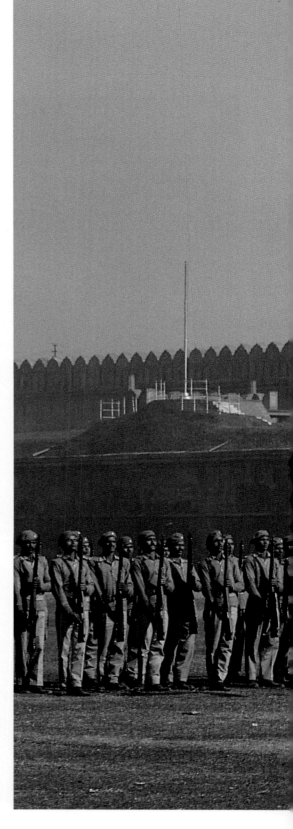

lighted by broad avenues, great domed administrative buildings, and a circular Parliament House. The new capital was officially inaugurated in 1931.

The Indian artisans and laborers who built these stately structures could later take pride in the fact that they had erected them for their own independent nation. The stimulating mixture of British and Indian efforts in creating the capital buildings–and the parliamentary system of government–is symbolized in the annual Beating of the Retreat ceremony ending the Republic Day celebrations. Ranks of Indian bagpipers march in procession within the government complex, and the noble Bikaner Camel Corps stands at attention on the ramparts, silhouetted against the setting sun.

Members of modern India's armed forces train in the shadow of Emperor Shah Jahan's seventeenth–century Red Fort. Crenelated battlements enclose lawns, elegant chambers, and a delicate marble mosque.

Strength of body and mind are ancient Indian values maintained by young men playing a game of kabaddi in a village outside Delhi. Such games have enhanced the skills of Indian farmers and warriors throughout history.

At the Beating of the Retreat ceremony ending the Republic Day celebrations, the Bikaner Camel Corps stands silhouetted against the setting sun.

On Republic Day, richly caparisoned elephants proceed down Rajpath, New Delhi's broad parade avenue, bearing musicians as well as citizens being honored for personal courage

Republic Day, January 26, is celebrated most grandly in New Delhi, where symbols of the great nation's military might and cultural wealth are displayed in what must be the world's most impressive parade. The orange, white, and green Indian flag flies all along the route.

At the time of India's annual January Republic Day celebration, New Delhi's government buildings are dramatically illuminated, lending the businesslike city the atmosphere of a fairyland.

Delhi women value time–honored traditions, but many engage in new occupations. These computer instructors are practicing their skills.

At Rajghat, near the banks of the Jamna River, a serene monument marks the site where Mahatma Gandhi was cremated after his assassination. Visitors come here to meditate on the man and the meaning of his life.

India Gate, a memorial arch honoring members of the Indian armies who fell in World War I, is one of New Delhi's imposing structures.

The national government of the world's largest democracy is headquartered in this Secretariat building and the other grand edifices of New Delhi, officially inaugurated in 1931.

Blossoms brighten the Panch Mahal building at Fatepuhr Sikri, an antique treasure of historic Uttar Pradesh.

The Mughal emperor Akbar the Great built his new capital of Fatehpur Sikri (City of Victory) about 1571. The beautiful red sandstone buildings remain in pristine condition even today.

Uttar Pradesh: Treasure House of the North
Agra: City of Wonders

Some 120 miles south down the Grand Trunk Road from Delhi, in India's most populous state of Uttar Pradesh (Northern State), rises the city of Agra, built along the banks of the Jamna River. A large metropolis boasting many industries, its streets are extremely busy. Numerous mills produce iron, cotton, processed lentils, and vegetable oils. In its lanes artisans bend over lasts, crafting shoes–Agra is second only to the city of Kanpur in the production of shoes. Yet Agra is known the world over not for its foodstuffs or footwear, but for its surpassingly splendid Mughal monuments.

During the sixteenth century, Agra became the capital and crossroads of the Mughal Empire. The great emperor Akbar, ruler of much of India, held court there. Queen Elizabeth of England, his contemporary, once wrote him a letter, hand–carried to him by three English traders. They found Agra "greater than London" and were very impressed by the sumptuous goods in the bazaars.

Akbar had a massive red–walled citadel built in Agra. The interior of the fort was later embellished with a white marble mosque and the Mirror Palace, its walls inlaid with tiny, dazzling mirrors. Truly the Grand Mughal, Akbar brought glory to Agra, yet he moved his capital outside the city to the village of Sikri.

Despite an impressive roster of military conquests and having access to a number of wives, Akbar had no son. Always a contemplative man, he visited a Muslim hermit in Sikri, and the emperor's prayers were abundantly answered. Before long, Akbar had three sons by different wives. Akbar selected this aus-

picious village for his new capital and oversaw the building of an exquisite complex of red sandstone buildings. With an army of workers on the job, palaces, halls of audience, gardens, baths, and a surrounding battlemented wall sprung up as if by magic. In delicate contrast to the rose–colored stone, a finely latticed white marble tomb was constructed to memorialize the saint. In celebration of yet another of his military triumphs, Akbar ordered the construction of a grand triumphal gateway and named his new city Fatehpur Sikri–City of Victory.

In 1588, barely fifteen years after the city was built, menacing affairs of empire in the northwest caused the emperor to shift his headquarters to Lahore (now in Pakistan). The glorious fairyland of red sandstone and white marble was abandoned, today still in almost pristine condition for visitors to enjoy. Unfortunately, the sons of one of the greatest monarchs in history proved to be base drunkards. It remained for Akbar's grandson, Shah Jahan (Ruler of the World) to bring even greater glory to Agra.

Curving floral motifs decorate pillars and brackets at Fatehpur Sikri, expressing the importance of both Hindu and Muslim influences in the growing Mughal empire.

The marble tomb of Saint Salim Chisti is embellished with a wealth of perforated marble screens. As they have for centuries, people hoping for the birth of a child come to offer prayers at the tomb.

The white marble tomb of Salim Chisti honors the saint whose blessings brought Emperor Akbar three infant sons. Akbar selected the village of Sikri for his capital because the saint resided here, a few miles outside Agra.

The Hall of Private Audience at Fatehpur Sikri is uniquely designed with a carved sandstone podium featuring radiating bridges. The powerful Emperor Akbar sat upon the podium, high above his courtiers.

Framed in the arch of its gateway, the beauty of the Taj Mahal is luminous.

The Taj Mahal

The silver light of the full moon shines upon its cool white dome, softly glowing in the night air. The quiet of the moonlit darkness is broken only by the small cries of night birds and by the haunting strains of an Islamic hymn sung by a worshipper, echoing inside the marble–walled tomb.

The extreme beauty of the Taj Mahal can be appreciated not only by subtle moonlight but in the radiance of dawn and the orange glow of sunset. Even in the brightest light of midday, this graceful white marble structure shines with awe–inspiring loveliness.

In 1628, Shah Jahan was proclaimed Emperor at Agra. His favorite wife, Mumtaz Mahal (Ornament of the Palace), was much beloved by this man who had once been capable of having his brother strangled. In 1631, Mumtaz Mahal died while giving birth to her fourteenth child. Shah Jahan was prostrate with grief and never married again. The sorrowing emperor had erected over her grave on the bank of the river perhaps the most beautiful monument in the world, the Taj Mahal (the Crown Palace).

For fifteen years over twenty thousand workers were employed in building the soaring structure, the apogee of Mughal architecture. The walled complex includes two mosques and an imposing gateway. In the center, framed by ornamental gardens and mirrored in a reflecting pool, rises the sublime vision of the domed mausoleum, adorned with four lofty minarets. Pointed arches accent windows and doors, while pierced marble screens filter the light. Graceful architectural details are highlighted with carvings of flowers and inlays of semiprecious stones.

Below the dome, in a dimly lit chamber, lie the mortal remains of the royal lovers. Shah Jahan had originally planned another tomb for himself—a black marble replica of the Taj Mahal, across the river, linked to the white monument by a silver bridge. Fortunately for the overtaxed populace, his dream was never realized. His power–hungry son, Aurangzeb, seized the throne and imprisoned him in the Agra Fort, where he spent his last days gazing from a balcony at the ethereal monument he had conceived for his lost love.

Three centuries later, endless streams of visitors from all over the globe come to experience the inspiring serenity of the Taj Mahal. It has been said, with undeniable verity, that the Taj Mahal is the miracle of miracles, the final wonder of the world, the jewel in India's architectural diadem.

Set within a Mughal garden, the Taj Mahal glows with the rosy light of dawn.

Delicate inlaid stone designs and calligraphy add elegant detail to the classic Mughal lines of the Taj Mahal.

Morning light shines behind the domes and minarets of the Taj Mahal, built on a platform high above the Jamna River.

Previous page: Sunshine reveals the mastery of those who built the Taj Mahal. The image of the grand monument shimmers in reflecting pools and canals.

The entrance to the Taj Mahal and its Mughal garden is guarded by a grand gateway of sandstone embellished with curvilinear inlaid patterns and Koranic verses.

Inside the Taj Mahal, the tomb markers of Queen Mumtaz Mahal and Emperor Shah Jahan are encircled by walls of marble tracery set with elaborate inlays of precious and semiprecious stones. The actual graves lie in a chamber below.

The domes and pavilions of the mosques framing the Taj Mahal are silhouetted against the orange glow of sunset.

Centers of Hinduism

Even as the Mughals were busy with their building projects and their imperial dramas of conquest and court intrigue, fired by a sometimes militant Islam, the Hindu culture of the masses of people around them remained remarkably resilient. Centers of Hindu worship and learning that had been sacred for thousands of years continued to be so, and Hindus quietly maintained their age–old relationships with their deities. Many of these sacred locales are highlights of a Hindu pilgrim's tour of North India.

Barely thirty miles from Agra, on the highway to Delhi and on the Jamna River, is Mathura, regarded as the birthplace of Lord Krishna, an incarnation of Vishnu, born perhaps five thousand years ago. Krishna is a greatly beloved god. He is said to have engaged in endearing childhood pranks, such as getting into the butter jar, as well as less childish activities, like stealing the clothes of damsels bathing in the river. His legendary amorous dalliances with milkmaids are taken as symbolic of the sacred bonds of love between deity and worshipper. Various miracles are also attributed to him, such as protecting the populace in time of calamity.

The very places where this passionately loved god carried out his life are visited by hosts of eager pilgrims, who travel to the prescribed locales around Mathura and nearby Brindavan. Bathing steps (ghats), shrines, and temples abound here, including the recently built temple of the International Society for Krishna Consciousness—"Hare Krishna" Western converts to Hinduism. The streets are filled with holy men, pilgrims, scribes, and would–be guides. Images of the happy blue–skinned god abound. Temple courtyards echo the pious hymn–singing of worshippers, including many widows. Ecstatic with devotion for Lord Krishna, pilgrims sometimes dance with the joy of feeling the presence of their Lord.

Allahabad, also known as Prayag, is normally a relatively quiet city. Situated on the flat land where the sacred Jamna River meets the even more sacred Ganga River, it is one of the most holy sites of Hindu pilgrimage. Here at the Sangam, or joining of the two rivers with the mythical Saraswati River, huge numbers of worshippers gather, particularly at the incredibly massive Kumbh Mela gathering, which draws millions. All rush to bathe in the holy waters at the most ritually auspicious moment.

Not only the scene of millennia–old rites, Allahabad is also the former home of the Nehru family, leaders of modern India. Their family mansion, now a museum, displays items from four generations of

The Kumbh Mela at Allahabad is attended by more people than any other single event on earth. Periodically, millions of Hindus assemble to wash away their sins at the confluence of three sacred rivers.

At Mathura, Lord Krishna's birthplace, women gather to sing hymns to the popular deity. Temple murals depict Krishna entrancing devotees with his flute and standing in a lotus–garlanded manifestation known as Srinathji.

Cremations on the riverbank mark the passing of those fortunate enough to end their earthly existence beside the Ganga. Dying at Varanasi is believed to help ensure release from the cycle of rebirth.

Practicing his morning yoga exercises on the waterfront steps beside the Ganga, a young man stays physically and spiritually fit.

A devotee rises to greet the dawn on the holy Ganga River at Varanasi, the Hindu City of Light. Varanasi is Hinduism's most sacred pilgrimage site and one of the oldest cities on earth.

astute politicians—Motilal Nehru, early advocate of independence; followed by Prime Minister Jawaharlal Nehru; his daughter, Prime Minister Indira Gandhi; and finally her late son, former Prime Minister Rajiv Gandhi.

Farther east, along the sanctified flow of the Ganga, stands Varanasi, the Hindu City of Light. Also known as Benares and Kashi (the Luminous), Varanasi is Hinduism's most sacred pilgrimage site. For thousands of years, the devout have come to spiritually cleanse themselves in the river at this location. The rich spirituality of Hinduism is displayed along the river bank and in the quaint lanes and crowded temples of Kashi, often dubbed Sukhada, or Bestower of Blessings.

According to myth, Lord Shiva appeared here in a fiery shaft of light, which rose up from the nether-worlds, broke open the earth, and pierced the roof of the heavens. Today's Kashi is seen as that very shaft of light, Shiva's holy lingam, or phallic symbol of energy, represented for human eyes in smaller stone images in temples and shrines.

Here, in this intensely sacred center, acts of religious merit, such as taking the sacred bath, giving to beggars, or offering gifts to Lord Shiva, are particularly fruitful. Dying in the eternal city of Varanasi is believed to lead to the salvation of the soul and freedom from the torturous cycle of rebirth. Simply being in Kashi for that moment of crossing over into the next phase of existence is said to bring eternal bliss.

This, then, is why Varanasi's lanes are filled with travelers and people—particularly aged widows—who have come to stay. This is why Varanasi's riverfront is crowded each dawn with bathers, praying, per-forming yoga, and dipping into the river's chill waters. Not far from the bathing areas are the cremation ghats, where the bodies of the many who have achieved their goal of passing away in Kashi are commit-ted to the elements. For the devout, queries about possible water pollution are irrelevant—the river is, by definition, religiously pure and purifying.

Pilgrims visit particular sites, not only the bathing ghats, but also several temples. The golden spires of the Viswanath Temple—dedicated to the Lord of the World—in the heart of the city beckon to Shiva's devotees. The temple dates from 1776; its ancient predecessor was razed by order of the Emperor Aurangzeb. The original Shiva lingam is said to be preserved in the newer temple.

Another eighteenth-century temple, dedicated to the Goddess Durga, is known as the Monkey Temple because of the horde of brash rhesus monkeys who clamber over its ocher-tinted walls. Varanasi's mon-keys snatch the eyeglasses and purses of pilgrims, sometimes even mischievously climbing to the tops of trees and tossing stolen coins into the river. Despite such distractions, for the pilgrims who have traveled from all across India, Kashi provides perhaps the most profoundly moving spiritual experience of their lives.

The region is sacred not only to Hindus, but to Buddhists as well. Only a few miles from Varanasi is Sarnath, where Lord Buddha preached his first sermon after attaining enlightenment. The remains of great stupas, which are masonry burial mounds, remind pilgrims of the heyday of Buddhism in India. A pillar carved with an edict by the Emperor Ashoka stands in front of the main shrine. A museum displays fine sculptures from the various periods of Sarnath—Mauryan, Gupta, and later.

Morning bathers gather at the ghats (bathing steps) in Varanasi to cleanse their bodies and souls in the waters of the holy Ganga. A bath here brings special religious merit.

Bathers dip in the waters of the Ganga, considered a goddess, sharing this timeless ritual of devotion with pilgrims from all over India.

About twenty–five hundred years ago, Buddha preached his first sermon at Sarnath, near Varanasi. The Dhamekh Stupa was erected fifteen hundred years ago at this site sacred to Buddhists.

Resplendent silk brocades are woven by modern Varanasi weavers, whose products are considered the epitome of luxury all over India.

Aflame with cosmic energy, Lord Shiva performs his dance of creation in a Varanasi wall mural. According to legend, Lord Shiva once appeared here in a fiery shaft of light, and he is the prime deity of the city.

Facing the river revered by untold generations of Hindus, a worshipper at Varanasi recites his morning prayers.

An ascetic holy man contemplates the sacred City of Light. His forehead is painted with three stripes of sandalwood paste, declaring his devotion to Lord Shiva.

Mountain Magnets

Most of Uttar Pradesh is plains, but the northwest segment of the state rises thousands of feet to the foothills and then to the Himalayas themselves. In contrast to the stunning heat of the plains in the hot season, these regions are cool and inviting, their snowy mountains and flowery meadows providing inspiration to religious and secular travelers alike.

Ardent Hindu pilgrims seek spiritual fulfillment in a visit to Hardwar, where the Ganga, rushing from the hills, meets the plains. A sacred bath there is particularly propitious. Nearby Rishikesh is also holy.

Higher in the mountains, surrounded by snow–capped peaks, is Badrinath, a Hindu pilgrimage center for untold centuries. Pilgrims often walk barefoot over snowy paths to reach the many temples and resthouses of this sacred spot. Kedarnath is another high–altitude pilgrimage site set amid snowy vistas.

Truly energetic worshippers can make the climb to Gangotri and Gaumukh, over 13,700 feet in elevation, where the River Ganga actually emerges from the Gangotri Glacier to begin its journey all across northern India.

Wild elephants roam among tall grass at Corbett National Park, India's oldest wildlife sanctuary, cradled in the northern foothills of Uttar Pradesh.

The mountains are magnets for all who wish to escape the heat of the plains. In the foothills of the Himalayas are famous hill stations, popularized by the British and now patronized by India's prosperous city dwellers on holiday. Dehra Dun, Mussoorie, Ranikhet, and Nainital are some of the towns offering cool breezes, forested vistas, and an unhurried atmosphere. Another attraction is Corbett National Park, close to the foothills, in Nainital District. The park is inhabited by elephants, tigers, leopards, and varieties of deer.

In northwest Uttar Pradesh, verdant foothills rise from the plains. Emerald–toned rice grows in elaborate terraces, cultivated by diligent farmers.

Still other travelers come to the mountains to trek and climb. Rich green forests and blossoming meadows are set off by glimpses of glistening glaciers and soaring peaks. India's loftiest mountain, Nanda Devi, over 25,400 feet high, is surrounded by 70 white peaks, beckoning dedicated climbers to seek their own special visions of paradise.

Bihar: Ancient Site of Inspiration

Visitors to the state of Bihar, just east of Uttar Pradesh on the Gangetic plain, may not find much to inspire them, unless they are seeking work in the cause of social and economic justice. Much of Bihar's dense population is busy eking out a living on fields controlled by landlords. An increasing number of people are finding employment in steel mills and other industries. The state is not adorned with ornamental architecture of the quality found in so many Indian regions.

Yet, in times past, Bihar was the site of crucial religious and political events that continue to interest thinkers of today. Some tribal people in the forested southern part of the state still follow traditional ways of life, although many now work in the new industrial cities, which have sprung up since independence. Bihar is also where a small but encouraging movement in folk art is taking place.

Patna, Bihar's capital, was for centuries capital of the huge Mauryan Empire, which controlled a large part of ancient India. From here, the great Emperor Ashoka commanded his realm from 274 to 237 B.C., setting an example of enlightenment scarcely matched for centuries. Examples of his pillars, topped by his lion symbol, remain to remind us of his virtues.

In Bodhgaya, Buddhist pilgrims venerate Buddha's enlightenment, said to have been attained under a Bo tree there. An actual descendant of that tree is growing in Bodhgaya today, having been propagated from a cutting from the original tree, taken to Sri Lanka and still flourishing there.

A major Jain pilgrimage center is Parasnath, atop a steep hill. Here a number of Jain tirthankars (saints) are said to have achieved nirvana.

In northern Bihar, in the region of the former Hindu kingdom of Mithila, villagers adorn their homes with exquisite paintings. On whitewashed walls, curving lines outline gods and goddesses, brides and grooms, flowers and tendrils, with accents of bright colors. In recent years, these beautiful paintings have been made on paper so that people outside the region can have access to them. Known as Madhubani painting (after the district in northern Bihar in which the majority of the painters live), the folk art has had a great commercial success. Most of the painters are women, but men are also joining in the perpetuation of this delightful tradition.

A young mother of the Mithila region of northern Bihar paints deities in vivid colors on the walls of her home—and on paper, so that others may have access to her delightful art.

Monsoon rains shower life onto lush rice fields near Bodhgaya in Bihar State. Bihar's cultivators lead lives of hard work and challenge.

Punjab and Haryana

Industrious farmers till the fertile land of these two flat, sunlit states. Abundant crops are their reward—impressive proportions of surplus wheat and rice are produced by these sons and daughters of the soil. Punjab's per capita income is fifty percent higher than the all–India average.

Punjab and Haryana share a common origin and a common capital. The Punjab region takes its name from the Persian panj (five) and aab (waters), referring to the land of five rivers. At the partition of India and Pakistan, the Punjab was divided between the two countries, and then in 1966, the Indian segment was divided again into the largely Sikh state of Punjab, the predominantly Hindu state of Haryana, and the mountainous state of Himachal Pradesh.

Chandigarh, a strikingly modern capital, was designed for the Indian Punjab prior to its 1966 division. Today, both the new, smaller Punjab and Haryana claim it, so the city houses the governments of both. Its wide boulevards and imaginative public buildings were planned by the French architect Le Corbusier and his associates. The attractiveness of the city is enhanced by many flowering trees, an extensive rose garden, and a visually intriguing park with statuary fashioned from broken pieces of crockery.

Amritsar, the holy city of the Sikhs, is the jewel of the Punjab. In the center of a sacred lagoon rises the Golden Temple, its gilded roof gleaming in the sun. The original holy book of Sikh scripture is installed in the temple's inner sanctum. A continuous stream of worshippers arrives at the temple, all devoted to their faith and proud of Sikh accomplishments.

Since the founding of the religion, the Sikhs have desired their own independent nation. In 1984, the Golden Temple was the scene of fierce fighting between Sikh separatists and central government forces. Heated dispute over this issue is currently a matter of tremendous concern to all sides.

Glittering fragments of glass bangles adorn figurines at Chandigarh's unique Rock Garden. The folk artist Nek Chand has used found objects to create an imaginative wonderland park in this planned city.

A stalwart Sikh displays marks of his religion—uncut hair and beard, turban, and steel bracelet—symbolic of his unswerving devotion to God and his community.

The Golden Temple at Amritsar in Punjab is the vital center of the Sikh faith. Worshippers cross the Pool of Nectar (Amritsar) by bridge to enter the gilded sanctuary, where their sacred book is enshrined.

Himachal Pradesh: Himalayan Enchantments

North of Uttar Pradesh, the state of Himachal Pradesh is a delightful lure to travelers, offering cool beauty and splendid vistas. Famous hill stations, lush valleys, and rushing rivers are framed by snow–capped mountains. In addition to the Hindu residents, who have much in common with the people of the plains, there are people of Tibetan heritage, Buddhists who practice a vivid version of that serene faith.

The state's capital, Simla, was summer capital of the entire country during British times. Rudyard Kipling has immortalized those days, when whole offices, complete with files tied up with red tape, would journey to the cool hills, while the rest of India sweltered on the plains below.

The Mall, where British couples promenaded, is still a busy place, now lively with throngs of Indian vacationers. Architecture reflects English influence, and the Viceroy's Lodge now houses the Indian Institute of Advanced Studies. The green slopes that so delighted the Britishers continue to invite visitors, who walk among rustling pines and rhododendrons.

The Kulu Valley is one of India's most entrancing locations. Old wooden temples, folk festivals,

Known as the Valley of the Gods, Kulu is famous for its annual Dassehra celebration. Happy crowds convey festively decorated images of some two hundred deities like these to a central area and join in folk dances and song.

The rushing Beas River—along with mountain peaks, lovely valleys, verdant forests, and invigorating air—creates an atmosphere of enchantment in Himachal Pradesh.

heavily ornamented women, blossoming apple orchards, and carefully tilled fields are all part of the valley scenery. Kulu is known as the Valley of the Gods, primarily because of its annual Dassehra celebration. At this autumnal festival, the images of some two hundred gods are gathered from temples all around the valley and brought down to the town of Kulu to pay homage to the deity Raghunathji. Each deity is transported in a colorfully garlanded conveyance by devotees who vie for the auspicious privilege.

The Kangra district is also one of the most charming valleys in the region. The well–known Kangra school of painting developed here. The hill station of Dharamsala is close to the snowline and is especially interesting because of the presence of Tibetan refugees, including His Holiness, the Dalai Lama. Tibetan worship, operas, and dances are performed frequently. The ancient culture of Tibet is kept alive in this Indian haven, even as Chinese occupation threatens it in its homeland.

Travelers seeking an almost mystical meeting with the mountains journey through the Rohtang Pass, at 13,200 feet, to reach the two valleys of Lahual and Spiti. Cut off from the rest of the world for much of the year, these valleys are surrounded by bleak and windswept landscapes. Tantric Buddhism, Tibet's religion, has been the belief system of the inhabitants for unmeasured time. Prayer flags flap in the wind. Women grease their hair with butter and wear it in a multitude of long plaits. Men wrap themselves in woolen gowns and carry Buddhist prayer wheels and silver–lined tea bowls.

Monasteries, known as gompas, house brightly painted Buddhist art treasures and scriptures. In these Himalayan regions, arable land is extremely scarce. While the oldest son of a family may be encouraged to marry and run the farm, younger sons often join monasteries. In some communities, fraternal polyandry is practiced–a set of brothers share one wife. Thus meager farmsteads are not threatened with overpopulation or fragmentation, and the fragile environment continues to support its people.

For the residents of the Himalayan mountains and valleys, life can indeed be challenging, especially during the winters. Hard work is an expected feature of life. But for those who need not earn a living from windswept earth, the region offers abundant enchantment.

At Narkanda village, not far from Simla, winter snow brings chilly charm to the foothills of the Himalayas.

The Himalayan black bear lives below the tree line in the mountainous zones of the northern and far eastern parts of India. It feasts on succulent fruits, honey, insects, and even an occasional domestic animal.

The beautiful Kulu Valley is part of the northern state of Himachal Pradesh. Farmers' houses and carefully terraced fields cling to the slopes above the Beas River.

Jammu and Kashmir: Paradise of the Mughals

The state of Jammu and Kashmir, north of Himachal Pradesh, is actually comprised of three separate regions, each with its own topography and cultural traditions. Different languages and even different gods are characteristic of each area.

Jammu is low-lying, inhabited by Hindu and Sikh farmers and herders. Although the rural folk struggle to make a living on the dry slopes of the Siwalik range, the town of Jammu is embellished with some fine temples and a museum of over five hundred delicately painted miniatures. The cave temple of Vaishno Devi, thirty–seven miles northwest of the city, attracts thousands of Hindu pilgrims each year. Despite its own charm, Jammu is primarily a transit point for people on their way to the fabled attractions of Kashmir.

The Mughal rulers thought Kashmir to be like unto paradise—and many modern travelers would agree, especially during the summer. While Delhi may be like an oven or a sauna in June or July, Kashmir offers the cool pleasures of refreshing breezes, flowing water, and uplifting mountain panoramas. The Mughals built their formal gardens here, with flower beds and water channels designed to delight the beholder. Until recently, many of India's romantic, swashbuckling films were made in Kashmir, with singing heroes and heroines tripping happily through gardens or mountain meadows. Unfortunately, recent political strife has been so disruptive that neither movie makers nor casual travelers can presently include the area on their itineraries.

Srinagar, Kashmir's capital, is set within the famous Vale of Kashmir, nestled below Himalayan peaks. Gingerbread–trimmed wooden houses line the banks of the Jhelum River, with the waters of Dal Lake close by.

Kashmir, an earthly paradise for Mughal emperors and modern travelers, radiates natural beauty. Snow–capped peaks, mountain meadows, and rushing streams offer cool contrasts to crowded hot lands to the south. Sonamarg is a favorite destination for visitors.

Everywhere there is water, and ordinary folk paddle small gondo-lalike boats called shikaras to and fro. The valley's lush rice fields are well irrigated. For visitors, instead of boring hotels, there are imaginatively named houseboats fitted out with every comfort. Moving from one houseboat to another, merchants paddling their shikaras vend roses, apples, finely embroidered cashmere shawls, woodcarvings, carpets, and ornately painted papier–mache boxes.

Most of Kashmir's population is Muslim, and several mosques proclaim the faith of the prophet in what was a Hindu–ruled kingdom before Indian independence. Kashmiri Brahmans, high–status Hindus, retain an elite demeanor. Prime Minister Nehru's family was of Kashmiri Brahman origin.

Since the days of the Mughals, catering to visitors has been a Kashmiri specialty. A prime pastime is a luxuriously serene ride in a private shikara across Dal and Nagin lakes. Green lines of chinar trees and blue mountain peaks are reflected in the calm

With water all around them, many Kashmiris live on houseboats. Visitors can also stay in luxurious floating private hotels trimmed with wooden gingerbread and distinguished by imaginative names.

waters. Other excursions include trips to Gulmarg, a resort town boasting a meadow of flowers and a view of distant Nanga Parbat (the Naked Mountain), and to Pahalgam, a site of majestic mountain scenery.

For many Indian travelers, Pahalgam is a staging area for the pilgrimage to Amarnath Cave, where a sacred pillar of ice is worshipped as a manifestation of Lord Shiva. For other Indians, golf is the lure—in fact, there is a nine–hole course at Pahalgam and an eighteen–hole course at Gulmarg. Fly–fishing and skiing are also great attractions. Trekking into the mountains is the goal of many visitors. For a great many summer visitors from the plains, the mountains of Kashmir provide their only experience of seeing and actually touching snow.

A florist paddles his boat bursting with vivid blossoms along a Kashmiri canal. Floating vendors bring houseboat dwellers every essential of life, as well as flowers, fine fabrics, and handicrafts.

The eastern segment of the state of Jammu and Kashmir is a spectacular arid plateau known as Ladakh. It is one of the highest regions on earth–much of it is over nine thousand feet high–and many peaks rise to dramatic heights. Ladakh is of military importance—it borders China, which has

attempted to grab the region–and is well defended by the Indian army. Because of its wild, rugged beauty, it holds a special place in the hearts and minds of those who have seen it.

Following the heart–stopping twists and turns of the road from Kashmir up to the Zoji La Pass brings one into another world. Gone are the verdant hillsides of Kashmir; instead, one sees an incredible moonscape of barren rock. The barrier of the Himalayas has effectively kept out many cultural influences, as well as all but a few inches of rainfall annually.

The Balti people follow Shia Islam, and the Dards are animists, practicing an ancient religion of their own. But most of Ladakh's people are Buddhists of the Tibetan tradition.

Historically, Ladakh has been linked with Lhasa, capital of Tibet. Monasteries own half of Ladakh's land, and many poor farmers are indebted to them. The many monasteries contain up to a sixth of the population.

The soil is thin, and fields must be carefully terraced. Barley, buckwheat, and wheat are grown, with both men and animals pulling the plows. Yaks as well as other animals are kept. Fraternal polyandry is

The Jhelum River flows through Srinigar, its banks lined with unique Kashmiri structures of wood and brick. A yellow–canopied shikara boat glides along the waterway, propelled by a heart–shaped paddle.

The Mughal Gardens of Srinagar, Kashmir's capital, offer lovely blossoms and fountains. At the Shalimar Garden, planted terraces rise to a marble pavilion designed for the pleasure of royal women of the 1600s.

At Leh's monastery, mountain winds ruffle lines of prayer flags, wafting human supplications to the heavens.

Women bow their heads in prayer outside one of Srinagar's major mosques. Their heads are covered with shawls and veils to show respect to God. Most Kashmiris are Muslims, although Kashmiri Hindu Brahmans comprise an important minority.

A young child learns his craft early in life. His small hands help weave a fine Kashmiri rug that may adorn a home anywhere in the world.

Kashmiri artisans create not only luxury goods but articles of ordinary daily life. This potter shapes common clay into useful bowls and vases. Throughout India, potters similarly practice their ancient craft.

Hand—embroidered flowers embellish a cashmere garment. Kashmiri embroideries, carved walnut wood, felt namda rugs, silks, and intricately painted papier—mache boxes are world—renowned.

Gloriously colored paintings decorate a door at Lamaruyu Monastery. In Himalayan Buddhist art, heroic saints and fantastic demons struggle in settings electric with cosmic energy.

A shepherd at Sonamarg lovingly cradles a lamb, part of the flock he tends. The wool of Kashmiri sheep and goats is woven into delicate shawls and rugs. Downy soft pashmina cashmere is made from the belly wool of Himalayan goats.

common here, with brothers sharing a wife or two, helping to keep the population density low.

Interestingly, cremation is favored, but the bodies of the poor are simply exposed to the elements, unless during their lifetime they have been able to accumulate a sufficient quantity of firewood, since wood is extremely rare in this barren region.

Pink granite, brilliant blue sky, clear air, and green valleys set off the windswept mountain peaks. Gompas (monasteries) perch on high cliffs, and chortens (stupas) and manis (sacred prayer stones) add ritual protection to the landscape. Walls of these stones may actually help protect from avalanches as well as from evil spirits.

The Indus River, so crucial to the development of Indian civilization in the lowlands, has its origin in these mountains. Above the Indus waters perches Ladakh's oldest monastery, Lamayuru Gompa, like a vision from a dream. Inside are figures of Buddha, colorful thankas (Tibetan devotional paintings on cloth), as well as monks and nuns clad in bright maroon and saffron robes.

Many other gompas, ancient and revered, are part of the striking Ladakhi landscape. At festivals, colorful masked dancers symbolizing good and evil perform in gompa courtyards. Crowds of spectators wear perky Ladakhi hats, woolen robes, and turquoise jewelry.

Leh, Ladakh's main town, was once an important commercial center on the Silk Road of Central Asia. Border problems have led to a cessation of this trade, and Leh is now a key military base. The Leh Palace and Temple of the Guardian Deities loom over the town.

Trekkers have a wealth of routes to choose from in this region. An especially remote destination is the Zanskar Valley, long and narrow and relatively little affected by outsiders. Conditions can be challenging, but the scenery is spectacular, with soaring snowy peaks piercing the brilliant sky.

East of Kashmir is the high Himalayan region of Ladakh, accessible via a mountain road of hairpin turns. Lush landscapes give way to rugged rocky beauty.

Fed by glaciers, the Indus River flows on its long journey to the warm plains of South Asia. Along its banks in Ladakh are mani stones carved with the prayers of Buddhist devotees. The stones take their name from the mantra Om Mani Padme Hum (Hail to the Jewel in the Lotus).

Like a vision of fabled Shangri–La, the Lamaruyu Monastery appears to have emerged from the mountain rock. The eleventh–century complex is considered the oldest in Ladakh and houses rich Buddhist art treasures.

Leh, Ladakh's capital, is set in the high valley of the Indus River. Outside the busy city are fertile fields and sacred sites. Rainfall is a sparse three inches per year.

Ladakh's remote, high–altitude Zanskar Valley shelters great natural and cultural beauty. Near the Suru River, the domes of a mosque gleam in bright light.

Ladakh's farmers must frugally husband their resources in this harsh land. Near Leh, the harvest of warm days is winnowed for feeding families during winter's icy season.

Rugged men of the Zanskar Valley enjoy a rough game of polo. In Ladakh, other amusements include archery and drinking barley beer or salty tea mixed with butter.

The Zanskar Range looms above Pensa La Glacier and a stone chorten, or stupa. The reliquary shrine commemorates a deceased lama or prosperous worshipper and offers auspicious protection to passersby in this spectacular land.

Celebrating a Buddhist festival, Ladakhi dancers wear traditional Tibetan-style woolen robes and silk scarves. Women display jewelry of heavy silver, gold, turquoise, and coral.

Maroon–robed monks dance at eight–hundred–year–old Thikse Monastery, atop a hill overlooking the Indus Valley. Monastery festivals are a focus of Ladakhi life.

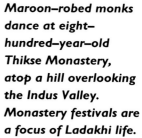

Festival crowds watch a fierce figure dance at a monastery celebration. In Ladakh, forces of evil are controlled by Buddhism's gentle but unswerving strength.

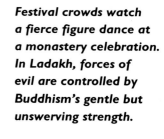

A young monk at Thikse exhibits the cheerfulness typical of the Ladakhi people. Most families contribute at least one son to the monkhood. Some small children show special signs that they are destined to become important lamas.

Royal Rajasthan

From far across the sere, dun–colored landscape, brilliant splashes of scarlet saris and golden turbans glimmer in the sun. Wild peacocks display their resplendent plumage. As the sun sets behind the domes of memorials to long–dead nobles, a string of ornamented camels stands silhouetted against the orange glow. And in the cool silence of a star–spangled desert night, within the weathered walls of a medieval fort, a bard sings plaintively of the heroes and heroines whose deeds brought glory to this historic land.

A Jaisalmer woman greets sunrise with a smile. The women of Rajasthan are famed for their beauty and tradition of honor. Some fought bravely in medieval wars, while others sacrificed their lives to save their honor.

Rajasthan

This is Rajasthan, literally, the Land of Princes, India's enchanting northwest desert state, known throughout the world for its noble traditions of valor and chivalry. Here exquisite palaces and glorious temples attest to the artistry of the people, while more than eighty forts stand witness to hundreds of harsh dramas of attack and defense. The traditions of Rajasthan were forged in the fire of the sun and the heat of battle.

Nature and geography have shaped Rajasthan's unique characteristics. In the east, the state is dry but still green in season, with hard–working farmers harvesting crops of grain, vegetables, and fruits from their carefully tended fields. Bisecting the state from south to north is the Aravalli Range, hills that effectively block moisture from reaching the western region, which tends to be very dry, and in the far west becomes the sandy Thar Desert. Winters and the monsoon season are moderate, but the summers can be infernos of searing heat. In these arid zones, meager crops and herds of sheep, goats, cattle, and camels must be kept alive with water brought to the surface from deep wells or preserved in reservoirs. Sources of water, fodder, and food are prime concerns for Rajasthan's rural people, the mainstay of the state's economy.

Rajasthan is in the path of the countless migrants, invaders, and traders who have entered India from the northwest. The region has been a crossroads of cultures throughout prehistory and history. Many have moved through this dry region with visions of the lusher, well–watered lands beyond, but many have stayed to mingle with those who came before, bringing new influences in from afar. Each fort and palace represents untold struggles, first of settlers, farmers, herders, and builders trying to eke out a living from the dry land, and then of rulers, attempting to achieve and maintain power, each in their turn challenged by rival chiefs and new invaders.

As people have continued to move into Rajasthan, others have moved out, because the arid land cannot support too many. Geographically, the area is large, but even with a population of forty–five million people, Rajasthan is the least densely populated of India's major states. Periodic droughts are constant threats. The farmers in some arid regions expect to move about during the driest parts of the year, seeking work for themselves and fodder for their herds. Migrant herders are a frequent sight along Rajasthan's roads, as the animals must keep on the move in an endless quest for vegetation. The gypsies of Europe and other parts of the world are Rajasthan's most famous emigrants—they long ago left this harsh area

A camel pulls a family's cart across the Rajasthani landscape, seared by the setting sun and by centuries of struggle.

A musician sings a plaintive song at desert Jaisalmer. Bards and musicians recite epic tales and sing ballads of Rajasthan's brave and tragic heritage, enchanting today's listeners.

Arid conditions keep animals on the move in search of fodder. Herds of sheep, camels, goats, and camels driven by turbanned men roam Rajasthan, endlessly seeking bits of greenery to sustain life.

Early light brightens a village homestead, molded of earth by sturdy sons and daughters of the land.

to make new lives far from their original homeland.

Rajasthan's earliest known inhabitants were the original tribal people of India, some of whose descendants still survive in the region. Later, settlements of the ancient Harappan civilization grew up here—archaeological remains have been found dating to about 2,200 B.C. A thousand years later, the horse–riding Aryan tribes began moving in from the northwest, bringing their Indo–Aryan languages and culture, including the beginnings of the caste system and the complex religion of Hinduism. About A.D. 400, Rajasthan became part of the great Mauryan Empire, stretching all across India, considered the most prosperous and civilized empire in the world at the time.

Then came more invasions and migrations, including the Huns and Scythians, each incorporated into the growing Indian society. During this period, the notion of the Rajput warrior caste developed. Rajputs—sons of princes—have been the respected nobility of Rajasthan for some fifteen hundred years. Their Hindu kingdoms flourished in northern India, especially the Rajasthan area, from A.D. 650 up to 1150.

The Rajputs believe that they are descended from the Scythians, superb horsemen and warriors. They are undoubtedly a mixture of many peoples and tend to be rather noble in their bearing. Rajput rulers claim descent from even loftier sources—from fire, the sun, and the moon. To this day, their clan names reflect this proud heritage. Chivalry and bravery remain revered Rajput traditions.

Interestingly, alongside the martial Rajputs developed a prosperous community of strictly nonviolent Jains. Industrious traders and merchants, the Jains built ornate temples that remain beautifully preserved. The protecting Rajputs and the commercially successful Jains have greatly benefitted one another.

A period of devastating raids from Afghan Muslims began in the eighth century, with the looting and destruction of villages, palaces, and temples taking a huge toll over hundreds of years. Forts and walled cities were built, attacked, plundered, and rebuilt. Time and again, marauders and even great Mughal emperors led their forces against the Rajput citadels. These clashes were violent in the extreme, sometimes ending with the Rajput women joining in a suicide pact to die in a huge fire (jauhar) rather than suffer the indignities of conquest, and the men fighting to their valorous deaths.

The tranquil light of dawn spreads over the Aravalli Hills in Rajasthan, India's driest state. The hills intercept moisture, thus helping to shape the Great Indian Desert to the west.

A couple load a cart with round cakes of dried cow dung to sell in Jaipur city. Dung cakes—virtually odorless—fuel the cooking fires of much of India. Wood is scarce and fossil fuels costly, while cow dung is abundant. Each patty is shaped by hand before it is dried in the sun.

Near Pushkar, men use camels to help pull water from their deep well. In dry areas, wells are often extremely deep.

A mainstay of Rajasthan's economy, a barefoot farmer tills his fields with a plow of ancient design. He depends upon his bullocks to help him wrest a living from the soil.

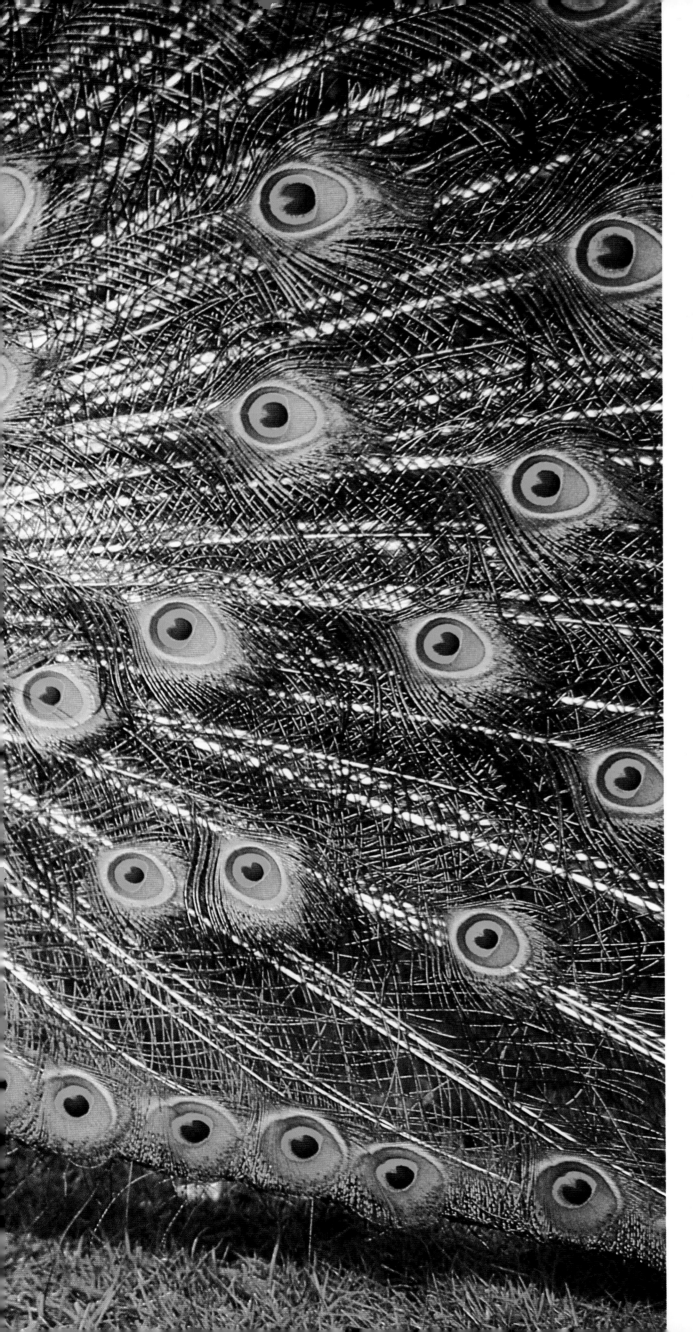

Happily bearing her headload, a woman of eastern Rajasthan carries water to her home. Typically, rural women fetch water from the village well at morning and evening, and a woman carrying a water pot on her head is considered a symbol of abundance.

Ultimately, the Mughals became the effective rulers of the region, with the Rajput princes having nominal authority in their separate princely states. Some of the great Mughals took Rajput princesses as wives, and three Mughal emperors—Jahangir, Shah Jahan, and Auranzeb—had Rajput blood in their veins. Only the royal house of Udaipur refused to give a princess to the Muslims, and to this day, Udaipur's Rajputs are deemed the noblest of them all.

After the decline of the Mughals, the British stepped in as the controlling force, with the princes officially ruling twenty–two states. Politics in Rajasthan remained stable thereafter, and at Indian independence in 1947, the states were merged with India. The region of the separate Rajput kingdoms became the modern Indian state of Rajasthan. The princes kept their property and titles until 1971,

A frequent sight in dun–colored Rajasthan are the iridescent displays of peacocks. The highly revered birds appear with haughty confidence everywhere throughout the state.

History is alive for the people of Rajasthan. Palaces and forts, like the Amer Fort at Jaipur, bespeak ancient deeds of valor and glory.

A cloth dyer stands before racks of saris tinted in vivid scarlet, destined to brighten the desert landscape. A love of bright colors is evident in Rajasthani women's dress.

Rajasthani men remember their warrior traditions of chivalry and valor. Use of opium was also a Rajasthani custom, still maintained in remote villages. These men perform a traditional ceremony of mixing and sipping opium tea.

when they were divested of these. Today they retain their titles purely as a matter of courtesy, and in an effort to remain solvent, many have opened their palaces as luxury hotels. Thus, visitors to Rajasthan can literally have the experience of living like royalty.

Throughout Rajasthan, there is a very strong sense of the turbulent past—of valor, fierce battles, elegant artistry, and thousands of years of history. Bards still sing of the ancient battles, and many of today's Rajputs proudly wear the brilliant turbans and sparkling saris of their ancestors. There are trains, taxis, and tractors everywhere, but camels, horses, elephants, and bullock carts are very much in evidence. Today, farmers, herders, builders, and merchants people the land, always with a splash of color. The Rajputs and the noble descendants of the ruling clans retain a proud position of honor. In Rajasthan, the past and the present come together in fascinating ways.

Water is treasured in Rajasthan, and ponds and wells are often ornamented with decorative pavilions and staircases. These women of Jaisalmer are filling brass pots with the vital fluid.

Maharaja Jai Singh II's interest in astronomy is revealed in the intriguing Jantar Mantar Observatory, a collection of structures carefully designed for making celestial calculations.

Jaipur, the City of Victory, is also known as the Pink City. In the eighteenth century, Maharaja Jai Singh II helped plan this fine capital. At the Palace of the Winds, ornate windows provided peepholes for secluded royal women.

Jaipur

Rajasthan's capital, in the eastern segment of the state, is now a large and bustling city, but it retains an antique charm. Its old city walls and many of its old buildings glow with a warm pink color. Maharaja Jai Singh II founded Jaipur (City of Victory) in the eighteenth century, enlisting the aid of a Bengali architect who brought together the best of Indian and international influences in the city's wide streets and rectangular blocks. Jai Singh's interest in astronomy is reflected in the observatory, Jantar Mantar, an intriguing collection of seemingly abstract structures designed for careful astronomical calculations. Jai Singh caused similar observatories to be built at Delhi and three other locations.

Jaipur's most famous landmark is the Palace of the Winds, or Hawa Mahal, a fantasia of 953 ornate windows set in a rose–colored five–story facade. From here, ladies of the court could look out at festival processions without jeopardizing their modest seclusion. Parades like those witnessed by those proper princesses still pass through Jaipur's streets on Hindu festival days.

The City Palace Museum houses a remarkable collection of textiles, paintings, manuscripts, and extraordinary weapons. On display are two huge urns of silver, said to be the largest silver vessels in the world. They once held a six–month supply of holy Ganga water for a Jaipur maharaja to drink while in London for the coronation of King Edward VII. Drinking water supplied by foreigners would have ritually polluted the orthodox Hindu maharaja.

High on the rugged hills outside of town sit ancient forts, including Amer (often called the Amber Fort), where the Jaipur royal house held court for seven centuries. Visitors riding painted elephants can ascend to the fort to see magnificent gateways, courtyards, pavilions, and a glittering chamber of inlaid mirrors. Along the way appear snake charmers and religious beggars with faces painted to make them look like living deities. After their journey into the past, the visitors can relax in luxury at the Rambagh Palace Hotel, where Jaipur's cosmopolitan Queen Mother, Gayatri Devi, resides in one wing.

A pride of peacocks adorn an ornate doorway in Jaipur's City Palace. Palace retainers stand at attention as in the past when Jaipur Court was headquartered here. The palace is now a fine museum.

An archway frames a delicately latticed structure within the Jaipur City Palace compound. Here one of the grandest of India's royal courts maintained valued Rajput traditions until very recent times.

Lord Ganesh, the elephant–headed deity who brings good fortune, presides over the doorway at the Amer Palace's Ganesh Gate. Like the princes of old, modern visitors to the fort–palace complex can climb the ramparts on elephant back.

Seated within the sacred space of a mandap (marriage booth) decorated with flowers, a royal Rajput couple at Jaipur sparkle with golden jewelry and embroidered silks. In the presence of royal guests from all over India, ancient rituals sanctify their union.

With the ancient Jaigarh Fort rising high above, the courtyards of the Amer Palace are awash with sun. Here fountains played and courtiers attended to royal needs for six centuries before the court moved to the site of Jaipur on the flatter land below.

Exquisite paintings decorate the walls and ceiling of the Darbar Hall at Samod Palace near Jaipur. The early nineteenth–century designs echo those on the fine carpet below.

Perhaps more than any other fort in Rajasthan, the great fort of Chittorgarh symbolizes the valorous traditions of the Rajputs. The walls still ring with the fierce battles fought here at the first capital of the royal house of Mewar.

Chittorgarh

About 150 miles southwest of Jaipur, the great fort of Chittorgarh stands atop a 500–foot high hill rising sharply from the surrounding plain. Today largely a deserted ruin, this fort perhaps more than any other symbolizes the honor and valor of the people of Rajasthan. Attacked repeatedly by invaders, three times it suffered the supreme sacrifice of the lives of all of its inhabitants. Despite the passage of centuries, the fierce struggles at Chittor are the subject of epic tales still told and songs still sung.

Chittorgarh became the first capital of the royal house of Mewar, descended from the sun, in the early thirteenth century. In 1303 the fort was attacked by Alauddin Khilji, the Sultan of Delhi, reputed to be interested in claiming the beautiful Rajput Princess Padmini as his own. If that was his goal, it was not to be realized, because as defeat became certain, Padmini and all the other women of the fort voluntarily committed themselves to the flames in ritual suicide. Their menfolk donned saffron robes and fought to their deaths.

Chittorgarh was later reclaimed by the Rajputs, but in 1535 the Sultan of Gujarat attacked. Again, thirteen thousand women died in the flames, and thirty–two thousand warriors died fighting. The fort was completely sacked. Barely thirty–three years later, the Mughal Emperor Akbar took the town. Despite a heroic defense, the odds were overwhelming, and thousands of women chose death before dishonor, while their defenders opened the gates to the fort and rode out to their deaths. Maharana Udai Singh fled to the site of Udaipur, where he established his new capital. In 1616, forty–eight years later, Emperor Jahangir returned the fort to the Rajputs, but they remained at Udaipur.

Today, massive fort walls, huge gateways, palaces, temples, and towers bear mute witness to Chittorgarh's turbulent past.

In the countryside outside Jaipur, red chilies dry in the sun. The hot peppers are arranged on rope–strung beds similar to those used by most Indians. Originally brought to India from the New World by the Portuguese, chilies are a common ingredient in Indian cooking.

At Jaipur, a young boy wears the garb of a sadhu, or holy man. His forehead is marked with Shiva's stripes, and his skin rubbed with sacred ashes. Shiva's trident is tucked into his topknot. Marigolds and holy rudraksha seed beads signify his special status.

Folk dancers smile with pleasure after a performance at Jaipur's Rambagh Palace. The brilliance of their costumes and the painted pots atop their heads are emblems of happy prosperity. Music and dance were traditional features of Rajput courts.

Udaipur

Among low–lying hills gleam the waters of Lake Pichola, created at the command of Udai Singh when he founded his new capital, City of Dawn, in 1567. On the banks of the lake rise many white buildings, including the multistoried City Palace, a complex of halls, chambers, towers, balconies, cupolas, courtyards, and galleries. On display in the palace, now a museum, are fine mosaics of peacocks, Rajasthan's favorite bird, miniature paintings of courtly life, and other precious objects. From the palace windows there are clear views of the Lake Palace, a white marble confection set in the center of the shining blue lake.

Approached by launch across the placid waters, the Lake Palace was built in the middle of the eighteenth century as the summer residence of the rulers (in Udaipur known as maharanas, not maharajas, as in the rest of India). Today the Lake Palace is a luxury hotel adorned with fountains, gardens, and even a swimming pool. It was featured in a recent James Bond adventure film. Some of its chambers glow with the jewel tones of stained glass and handpainted murals. At evening, its courtyards echo with the happy songs of folk dancers and musicians.

Old Udaipur's lanes are a charming profusion of whitewashed homes decorated with frescoes of elephants and deities, small shrines to Hindu gods, Jain temples, and a large temple to Vishnu as Jagannath, Lord of the Universe. Bazaar shops flash with the colors of silks, embroidered cottons, silver, gold, and precious gems. At auspicious times, wedding parties dressed in brilliant silver–trimmed garments parade through the streets, their joyous purpose announced by trumpets and drums.

The emblem of the radiant sun is emblazoned on royal objects at the court of the rulers of Mewar. The royal lineage is believed descended from the sun itself, and their capital is named Udaipur, City of Dawn.

The symbol of the sun goes before him as a Maharana, or King, of Mewar rides in royal procession with a queen. This modern painting continues in simple form the charming traditions of Rajasthani miniature painting.

Inlaid on the lower portion of the walls of the Crystal Room at the Shiv Niwas Palace are designs in colored glass. Here glass lions attack their prey while others peacefully recline.

Now a gleaming luxury hotel, the Lake Palace is approached by launch across the lake's calm waters. The hills beyond were once lushly forested but today are almost bare of trees.

The City Palace of Udaipur's rulers is the largest in Rajasthan. This imposing complex of ornate halls, courtyards, and apartments overlooks the cooling lake. To the left, upon its wall, an emblem of the Sun King shines.

The Shiv Niwas Palace was built in the late eighteenth century to house special guests of Maharana Fateh Singh. Its most lavish chamber sparkles with crystal furniture and chandeliers.

Reflections of whitewashed cupolas and arches shimmer in the waters of Lake Pichola at Udaipur. At left, steps leading to the water's edge provide places for bathing and washing clothes.

Baneshwar Fair

Every winter a unique tribal fair is held about seventy-five miles south of Udaipur, on a sandy delta formed by the joining of the small rivers Som and Mahi. At this confluence, some fifty thousand Bhils and other tribal people throng together to worship the Hindu deities enshrined in small temples. At dawn they bathe in the cold river water, cleansing themselves of sin. People whose relatives have recently died consign the ashes and scroll-like horoscopes of the deceased to the waters. After fulfilling these solemn and ancient duties, the mourners join other fairgoers in buying items at the merchants' stalls and meeting friends and relatives. In the evening, by the light of the full moon, at their campsites in this otherwise uninhabited spot, they join in hymns and folk dances.

The visage of a village elder reflects the determination of Rajasthan's people as they have met the challenges of the centuries.

A light intoxicant, betel leaf (pan) awaits buyers at the Baneshwar Fair. The leaves are spread with lime and sprinkled with aromatic spices to add to the pleasure of the chew.

South of Udaipur, the winter Baneshwar Fair attracts thousands of tribal folk to worship at small temples and bathe in sacred waters. Dawn light beams on devout pilgrims seeking divine grace.

Hymns in White Marble

Within the Ranakpur Temple, 1,444 intricately carved pillars support 80 domes and 44 spires. Saffron–robed priests guide the rituals of visiting worshippers.

A most serene side of Rajasthan is revealed in the exquisitely carved white marble temples of the Jains. Nonviolent worshippers of a series of incarnations of austere saints, the Jains maintain their antique religious edifices with love and care. Professional stone carvers are on hand to restore any sculptures worn by time or human touch.

About sixty miles west of Udaipur, high in the hills at the lakeside resort town of Mt. Abu, are some of the world's most beautiful carvings. They adorn the Jain Dilwara temples, inspiring testaments to an ancient and gentle faith. Rather plain on the outside, the temples burst forth in a profusion of sculptured imagery inside.

The Vimal Vasahi Temple, built in A.D. 1031, is dedicated to the first Jain tirthankar, or saint, Adinath. The saint's image is posed simply, in serene meditation, but the rest of the temple is embellished with curvaceous white marble lotus buds, birds, lions, dancers, musicians, worshippers, gods, goddesses, scrollwork, and a multitude of other representations. Lacy columns and arches surround the awed visitor. Marble latticework and quarter–size elephant sculptures complete the scene.

Sculptured marble ceiling panels at the Ranakpur Temple portray graceful deities, woodland spirits, and prayerful devotees.

Nearby, the Luna Vasahi, or Tejpal Temple, is another splendid house of worship, built in 1230. This exquisitely wrought structure is dedicated to the twenty–second Jain saint, Neminath. The intricately carved domed ceiling portrays animals, musicians, and deities in carvings so fine the stone seems almost transparent. The astonished visitor can only wonder how such delicate perfection could have been achieved.

Another complex of Jain monuments stands at Ranakpur, located a few miles to the north. In an isolated setting among the wooded Aravalli Hills lie the superb Chaumukha (Four–Faced) Temple and a few smaller temples and shrines. The main temple was built in the middle of the fifteenth century, and like the Dilwara Temples, is adorned with an abundance of intricate carvings. The temple's roofs and domes are supported by 1,444 pillars, no two of which are alike. Priests garbed in saffron robes grind fragrant sandalwood to make a paste to offer to Lord Adinath. Flowers and gold leaf are other favorite offerings.

The awe–inspiring temple complex is not just an architectural monument; Jain faithful journey here in large numbers every year, and free vegetarian meals prepared with the purest ghi (clarified butter) are provided to visitors by wealthy patrons of the temple.

The Jain temples of Rajasthan are exceedingly beautiful, expressing a nonviolent faith strongly contrasting with the values of the martial Rajputs. The Chaumukha Temple at Ranakpur has ornamented a serene glen in the Aravalli Hills for over five hundred years.

Ajmer

Southwest of Jaipur, near Rajasthan's center, is the city of Ajmer. Founded by Hindus and conquered alternately by Muslims and Hindus for centuries, Ajmer is the site of the sacred tomb of the great saint Khwaja Muinuddin Chisti, the most sacred of all Muslim places of pilgrimage in India. Born in Persia in the twelfth century, Chisti became a Sufi mystic and went to India as a missionary. He settled in Ajmer, then under frequent attack from Afghan invaders, and calmly established a moral code of conduct among his disciples.

Attributed with great powers, the deceased saint's tomb attracted Emperor Akbar as a supplicant more than three centuries later. Akbar sought a son and heir, and through the blessings of a member of the Chisti order at Fatehpur Sikri, finally got his wish. Akbar not only moved his capital to Fatehpur Sikri, but he honored the Ajmer saint with a grand mosque.

A six–day fair commemorating the Muslim saint's death anniversary is held each year. Thousands of followers arrive at the ornate mosque and tomb to admire the elegantly engraved silver panels, fine marblework, and the tomb itself, where prayers may bring boons. Donors provide food, which is cooked in enormous cauldrons and distributed free of charge to the respectful pilgrims. The food symbolizes the abundance of God's blessings. Those who eat the food prepared in one common pot feel a sense of unity with Muslims from all over India.

At Ajmer, near the center of Rajasthan, the revered tomb of the Muslim saint Khwaja Muinuddin Chisti draws thousands of pilgrims annually. Silver panels beautifully embossed with ornate floral patterns ornament the saint's tomb.

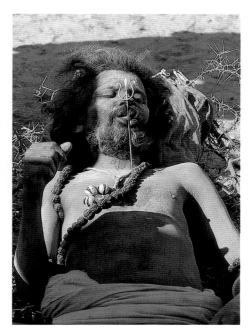

Among the Pushkar Fair's attractions are holy men from many parts of India. This ascetic has pierced his tongue with a trident, symbol of Shiva, and is lying on a bed of thorns. His skin is rubbed with holy ash. Through his austerities, he hopes to gain spiritual strength.

Pushkar

A few miles north of Ajmer is the sacred town of Pushkar (Lotus), situated on the shores of a jewel–like glacial lake. Dun–colored temple-topped hills and sandy fields surround the town. Normally quiet, Pushkar sees a small but steady stream of visitors to its temples and wide bathing steps leading down to the lake. But once a year, at the time of the full moon in November, the town explodes with colorful crowds of hundreds of thousands of pilgrims.

The great Pushkar Fair has become an internationally known attraction, and justifiably so, since it is one of the world's most dazzling trad-itional gatherings. Mentioned in the two–thousand–year–old Mahabharata as India's foremost pilgrimage site, Pushkar was also described by the eleventh–century Islamic scholar Alberuni as a place of high veneration for Hindus. Thus, the brilliantly garbed pilgrims who

Pushkar has been a sacred site of pilgrimage for at least two thousand years. At dawn on the Full Moon Day, bathers dip in the holy waters of the lake, which is said to have been created by Lord Brahma himself when he cast a lotus blossom to earth.

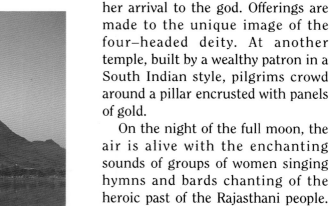

Hoping for divine blessings, women ornamented with jewelry of gold, ivory, silver, and mirror–studded lacquer bathe in the chilly waters of the sacred lake.

Pushkar's sacred lake is set amid the arid hills of the Marwar region of central Rajasthan. Its shores are studded with bathing steps and small temples.

come to Pushkar to bathe on the most auspicious bathing day of the year are following age–old traditions that will undoubtedly continue far into the future. Visitors can only watch in wonderment as the pageant unfolds.

For the five days leading up to the full moon, the crowds begin to gather. All around are exuberant faces amid a sea of bright hues and shimmering ornaments. Among the crowds are large numbers of turbanned Rajputs and their gilt–veiled womenfolk. Members of other groups wear distinctive costumes.

At their sandy campgrounds on the outskirts of town, the pilgrims cluster around campfires, cooking picnic suppers. Huge numbers of camels and cattle are on hand, and men examine the animals and dicker over sale prices. Traders' stalls draw hundreds of customers buying camel saddles, embroidered horse decorations, hand–forged daggers, snacks, bangles, ribbons, metal storage chests, and wooden pitchforks. Freak shows and ferris wheels attract hundreds of patrons. In the evenings, capacity crowds throng to huge theater tents to enjoy traditional musical dance–dramas in the Marwari regional language.

But the serious business of Pushkar is the pilgrimage. Worshippers crowd into the Brahma Temple, one of perhaps two or three temples in all of India dedicated to this divinity. Each visitor reaches up to ring a bronze bell announcing his or her arrival to the god. Offerings are made to the unique image of the four–headed deity. At another temple, built by a wealthy patron in a South Indian style, pilgrims crowd around a pillar encrusted with panels of gold.

On the night of the full moon, the air is alive with the enchanting sounds of groups of women singing hymns and bards chanting of the heroic past of the Rajasthani people. Then, in the chill hours before dawn, a great spectacle begins. In the dark, crowds of people wend their way through the narrow lanes down to the bathing steps. Through morning mists, the golden light of the rising sun illuminates the fair's crescendo: thousands upon thousands of devout bathers moving to the water's edge all around the lake. In the cold air, they doff much of their heavy drapery, quickly bathe in the chilly water, and dress again. With the completion of their baths in the sacred waters, hopes of salvation are raised, and a deep sense of community with pilgrims of the past and present is enhanced.

Their spiritual duties fulfilled, the fairgoers enjoy the afternoon at competitions in camel racing, horsemanship, and tugs of war. Spectators roar at camel strength contests, in which the braying beasts are loaded with as many riders as they can bear. The overloaded animals stubbornly drop to their knees, dumping their riders in hilarious heaps.

Finally, the throngs of happy pilgrims pack their bundles and head home, their hearts overflowing with memories of holy Pushkar and their spirits filled with peace.

Every November, thousands of rural folk gather at Pushkar for the great Pushkar Fair, where camels and cattle are traded and ancient Hindu practices are observed.

Worshippers crowd into Pushkar's temple of Lord Brahma, the largest of perhaps two or three in all of India dedicated to this august divinity. Devotees press forward to see the unique image of the god.

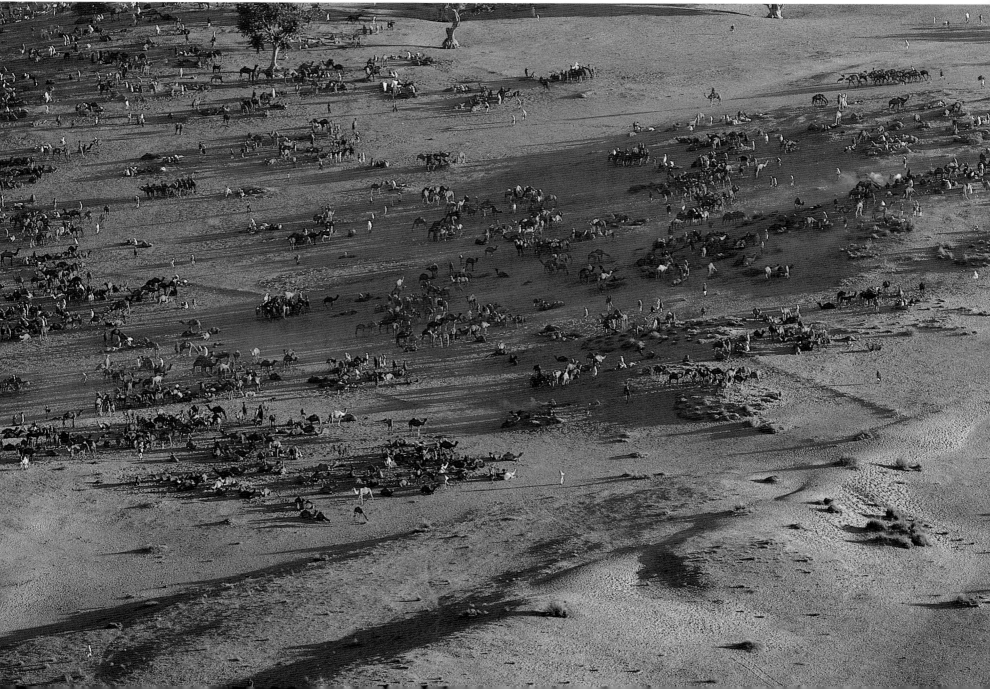

Village men laugh with hilarity at camel strength contests. The animals are loaded with as many riders as they can bear, and when they have had enough, they fall to their knees and dump the riders off.

Urged forward by their enthusiastic riders, camels race across the Pushkar sand. The camels are decorated with patchwork saddle pads, painted designs, and patterns trimmed into their hair.

A rustic folk image of the Goddess Kali attracts contributions from villagers who desire her blessings. This fierce goddess can control life, and her garland is strung with the heads of her enemies.

Seven miles from Pushkar, a train at Ajmer's station is jammed with villagers heading home after the fair. India's train system is vast and effectively conveys passengers all over the nation.

At Jodhpur, the imposing Meherangarh Fort towers four hundred feet over the city. A series of walls and gates renders the majestic five–hundred–year–old compound all but impregnable.

A royal chamber inside the Jodhpur Fort displays painted and gilded walls, a charming cradle, a flapping ceiling fan to be pulled to and fro by a servant, and a brocade cushion against which the ruler might rest while playing a game of parcheesi.

Just inside a gateway to Jodhpur's fort are carved stone handprints of women. These honor the memory of Rajput widows who honorably died in their husband's funeral flames. The handprints are regularly worshipped with applications of silver leaf and garlands, since women who died in this self–sacrificing way are considered saints.

The Umaid Bhawan Palace was created in the twentieth century for the pleasure of the Maharaja of Jodhpur. Today the ruler and his family live in one section, while the rest of the palace is a grand hotel.

Jodhpur

Traveling west from Ajmer across dry landscape for one hundred miles, one reaches Jodhpur, with its impressive Meherangarh Fort towering four hundred feet above the city on a mighty eminence. Inside the rugged walls and lofty gateways are a series of lovely buildings, some ornamented with finely carved windows and fretwork. Exquisite decorations and paintings beautify some rooms. These delicate touches are offset by displays of armor and weapons, as well as the poignant carvings of handprints at the entrance to the fort. These honor the memory of Rajput widows who immolated themselves on flaming pyres.

Visible from the fort's ramparts, far across the lively city, is the Umaid Bhawan Palace, built between 1929 and 1942 at the command of Jodhpur's maharaja. Four thousand workers labored to create this massive domed structure of reddish stone, designed by British architects. Once one of the largest private residences in the world, it is now primarily a luxury hotel, with one sumptuous wing reserved for the erstwhile royal family.

The shops of Jodhpur's bazaars display a delightful assortment of modern and traditional goods. Painted pottery, tie–dyed saris, jewelry, handicrafts, and antiques abound, along with vegetables, fruits, and zesty prepared foods.

From the fort, there is a breathtaking view of the city of Jodhpur and the dry lands beyond. Dominating the horizon at the edge of town is the Umaid Bhawan Palace, built as one of the largest private residences in the world.

Bikaner and Deshnok

Not long after Jodhpur was founded in the fifteenth century, a younger brother of the ruling house was urged to seek his fortune to the north. He did so, founding Bikaner in 1488. From this barren landscape emerged the remarkably beautiful Junagarh Fort, lavishly decorated inside with mirror work, carvings, paintings, and colored glass. Gilt reliefs and glass mosaics adorn some chambers. A prize exhibit is the Pugal, a seventh-century carved sandalwood throne, probably the oldest piece of furniture surviving in India today. It represents the power of the ruling family, deeply rooted as it is in historic tradition.

Visitors to Bikaner can stay at the pleasant Lalgarh Palace, where the royal family still resides. An impressive camel breeding farm also attracts visitors. But the most unusual sight in the Bikaner area—or perhaps all of India—is the Karni Mata Temple at Deshnok, a few miles to the south.

Karni Mata lived at Deshnok some five hundred years ago and is believed to have performed many miracles. To help thwart the God of Death, she arranged for the souls of deceased villagers to inhabit the bodies of rats. Similarly, when a local rat dies, it is reborn as a child in the village. The pretty carved marble temple to the goddess and its walled courtyard are consequently filled with hundreds of rats, who are treated kindly and fed fine foods. Visitors to the temple ought not to mind if curious rats tickle their toes, for are these rodents not actually incipient children, protected by a kindly goddess?

Karni Mata, a protective goddess of the Bikaner region, is revered at the Deshnok Temple. Within the temple precincts, rats are regarded as human souls under her care and are offered fine foods and gentle treatment.

To the west of Jaisalmer, where settlements are few and far apart, camels and their riders trek across the desert dunes.

112

Jaisalmer and the Desert

Long dry desert roads link Jodhpur and Bikaner with Pokaran to the west. From there, a single road stretches farther west into the Great Indian Desert, or Thar Desert, passing sandy flatlands, scrubby vegetation, browsing camels and goats, and mud–walled villages.

Viewed from the road, the villages appear uninviting. But at closer view, they are actually quite pretty. The earthen walls are shaped by hand, and houses are capped with jaunty peaked thatched roofs. Some houses and granaries are decorated with charming white designs. Women in ivory bangles, gold nose rings, and red headcoverings bring water from wells, while others sitting in cozy courtyards spin wool yarn. Men in white clothing topped by scarlet turbans are out herding their animals, endlessly on the move in their eternal quest for nutriments. In season, men and women tend their crops of grain, vegetables, and red chili peppers.

Continuing along the road to the west, one finds the serenity of the landscape broken only by the surprising sight of a brilliant peacock or the swift movement of a desert antelope. And then, rising from the sands in what seems to be a mirage, is the great fortress city of Jaisalmer.

Words can hardly capture the special enchantment of Jaisalmer. Its golden sandstone walls and bastions rise high above the surrounding land, forbidding, yet inviting to the traveler. Imposing gateways allow entrance into the only fort town in India still fully inhabited by an active community. This is no mere historic relic of bygone days; this is desert life as it is being lived today.

The golden city of Jaisalmer grew in prosperity because of its strategic location on the ancient camel train routes between India and Central Asia. Land trade was vital for centuries, and merchants and townspeople became wealthy. The fort, built in 1156, encloses mansions and fine Hindu and Jain temples, all financed with the profits from trade. The fort was attacked several times, and historic legends describe three occasions when hundreds of women died in the fiery

The Great Thar Desert stretches across western Rajasthan, its harsh sands providing little to feed people and their animals. Here hardy goats move across a dune, their herders carrying laboriously gathered fodder on their heads.

Rising from the desert sands are the ramparts of the majestic walled city of Jaisalmer. Medieval battles here claimed the lives of thousands of warriors, as well as those of their womenfolk, who preferred death to dishonor.

jauhar. For these, the inhabitants of Jaisalmer were not entirely blameless, since in the early history of the town, before the rise of the merchants, Jaisalmer's warriors sometimes ambushed treasure caravans winding across the desert, thus inviting return attacks.

The expansion of trade by ship and the growth of the port of Bombay led to Jaisalmer's demise as a trading center. However, the city retains its medieval atmosphere and attracts a growing number of visitors. Streets paved with golden–hued stone lead up through the fort, past charming shops, to the elaborately sculptured Jain temples at the apex of the town. Larger buildings of carved stone reflect golden light onto homes decorated with colorful folk paintings. But perhaps most entrancing are the elaborate mansions (havelis) of the rich and powerful of the past. The Patwon's Haveli is magnificently adorned with filigree–trimmed windows and interior murals. Nathmal's Haveli and Salim Singh's Haveli, both residences of former prime ministers of Jaisalmer state, are delightfully embellished with sculptures and carved wooden trim.

On the outskirts of the town stand memorials to deceased nobles as well as water reservoirs crowned with pavilions, ornamental tributes to the value of water in this desert land. Camels carry riders and pull carts, their special strengths vital to human prosperity in this arid zone. Past the horizon to the west, dunes of sand shift restlessly, blazing hot in the midday sun but subtle and inspiring in the rosy glow of sunset.

The commercial success of Jaisalmer's merchants is revealed in the beautiful mansions they had built for themselves. At the Nathmal family mansion, incredibly ornate carvings adorn the windows.

Everywhere in Rajasthan, water is highly valued, but nowhere more than at desert Jaisalmer. Just outside the city walls, a pond is lovingly adorned with temples and pavilions.

Jaisalmer prospered as a trading center in centuries past and today remains a market town. Here merchants vend a plentitude of vegetables beside the city wall.

On a hill overlooking the desert city, the serenity of sunset touches the memorial pavilions of past generations of Jaisalmer's nobles.

A young girl performs a traditional folk dance, her skirt whirling with bright colors against the backdrop of an earthen wall high within the fort complex at Jaisalmer.

At the gloriously beautiful Ranthambhor National Park in eastern Rajasthan, tigers stalk the jungle. After a period of strong decline, India's tiger population is on the rise again—there may now be as many as four thousand wild tigers in the country.

The Rajputs and their British guests enjoyed hunting Rajasthan's abundant wildlife. Fortunately, a splendid population of animals remains in the state's nature preserves. Here, a nilgai (blue bull), the largest of all Asian antelopes, looks up from its grazing at Keoladeo Ghana National Park.

Wildlife Wonders

The magnificent battlements of Ranthambhor Fort tower above the trees and vines of a great jungle sheltering an abundance of wild animals. Ranthambhor National Park in eastern Rajasthan is one of the best places in the world to view wild tigers and many other creatures. The presence of the ruined fort on a rocky hill high above, as well as antique pavilions below, give the area a haunting fairytale quality.

The ancient Chauhan Rajput fort was conquered by Alauddin Khilji in the fourteenth century, and again by Emperor Akbar in 1569. The clash of Mughal and Rajput armies was recorded in paintings in the Akbar Nama, the official chronicle of Akbar's reign.

Today, only small numbers of forest–dwelling people and wildlife enthusiasts remain to challenge the dominion of the tigers, who roam the forest and ruins with increasing confidence. Since 1972, when it was estimated that Ranthambhor's tigers numbered fourteen, Project Tiger has encouraged protection of the animals, now estimated at more than forty. These regal cats can be seen caring for their cubs, lounging in forest thickets, stalking sambar deer, and challenging crocodiles for prey.

Other Ranthambhor animals include spotted deer, panthers, hyenas, jackals, sloth bears, nilgai antelope, and wild boars.

An abundance of birdlife is found at Ranthambhor as well as at nearby Bharatpur (Keoladeo Ghana) National Park. Here over 350 avian species find refuge in woodlands and shallow lakes artificially created in the nineteenth century by order of the local maharaja so that he could enjoy a private shooting preserve. Now a protected sanctuary, the park is aflutter with an astounding array of permanently resident and migratory birds.

The black–faced langur monkey is a common sight in forested areas of Rajasthan. Often, the monkeys fearlessly beg for handouts from human passersby. They also helpfully groom domestic cattle and buffaloes.

The calls of hundreds of species of birds ring out at sunset at Keoladeo Ghana Park. Once a maharaja's private shooting preserve, the wetland park is now one of the finest wildlife sanctuaries in India.

The moon seems balanced on the ruin of an ancient arch at the deserted city of Mandu, high on a plateau in the Malwa region of Madhya Pradesh. Centuries of occupation by both Hindu and Muslim rulers left their marks at this haunting site.

The Arabian Sea washes the shore at Somnath, in Gujarat, where a new Hindu temple replaces previous temples sacked by invaders. The temple on this site a thousand years ago was incredibly wealthy and employed a thousand priests in the daily worship of Lord Shiva.

The Vibrant West and Central Heartland

Gujarat, Madhya Pradesh, and Maharashtra–three large states–together make up much of India's vibrant heartland. They shelter monuments of some of the greatest epochs of early Indian history and are also throbbing with active modern life. Fertile soils and minds combine to produce food surpluses, growing industries, and successful commerce. Yet India's ancient traditions play an active role in the lives of the people. Gujarati, Hindi, and Marathi are the primary languages of the area.

Gujarat: Cradle of Cultures

Gujarat, India's westernmost state, has a long coastline on the Arabian Sea. Geographically facing outward, Gujarat has welcomed an enormous variety of cultural influences from many lands. But Gujarat has not only taken in foreign influences; it has created its own rich traditions that have affected the world. Mohandas Gandhi was born here, and his ideas of nonviolence affected civil rights struggles in many parts of the globe. Gujarat is also home to communities known for their intellectual and commercial acumen. Members of these communities run businesses and practice professions in many countries. The products of Gujarat, particularly textiles, are to be found in virtually every nation on earth.

Ahmedabad

Ahmedabad is Gujarat's premier city, built in a region long settled. Just a few miles out of town is the ancient Harappan site of Lothal, once a port with probable trading links to Mesopotamia and Egypt. All around, fertile farms yield abundant crops and dairy products. In the city, delicate stone traceries at the Sidi Saiyad Mosque date from but a few years after Ahmedabad's founding in 1411. Unique step wells with subterranean sculptured stairways leading down to deep water sources were built in the city and its environs centuries ago. Mosques and temples of every age bespeak the city's multiethnic heritage. Gandhi's ashram, a modest structure at the edge of town, was once the vital nerve center of the Indian independence movement–a force that shook the mighty British Empire.

The vigor of Gujarat's handicrafts and textile industries is revealed in Ahmedabad's folk art museums, as well as in the justly famous Calico Museum sponsored by the Sarabhai textile family—who also supported Gandhi's activities. Here rich textiles are displayed alongside antique woodcarvings in a serenely beautiful manor set in a lush garden.

Following in Gandhi's footsteps, modern social reformers work with Ahmedabad's hardworking poor to help them create better conditions for themselves. The Self–Employed Women's Association (SEWA) is world-renowned. Modern institutions of research and higher learning are bubbling with intellectual activity. Factories, mills, and businesses of every sort are thriving. Ahmedabad is a city of industrious achievers.

Traditional Gujarati life is evoked at the Vishalla Restaurant and Vechaar Utensil Museum, just outside Ahmedabad. The museum displays hundreds of traditional domestic metal vessels and utensils; the restaurant serves vegetarian Gujarati favorites in a rustic, villagelike setting. Tangy curries, fresh hot breads, vegetables, and fresh fruits are served by friendly waiters in traditional Gujarati garb. Thus, in the midst of one of India's greatest centers of industry and trade, the old is preserved and enjoyed.

Flags of faith fly atop a small temple in Junagarh District, southwestern Gujarat. Brilliant pink bougainvillea blossoms frame the well–kept temple garden dotted with small white marble figures of deities.

Lord Ganesh, with his curving trunk, is the central figure in this folk embroidery. Sacred cows flank the deity. Gujarati women are famed for their intricate needlework glittering with tiny mirrors.

Cherished Towns and Countryside

Other key cities of Gujarat include Baroda (now called Vadodara), where the former maharaja's ornate palace brims with memorabilia; Gandhinagar, the state capital; Surat; Rajkot; and Junagarh.

Much of Gujarat consists of Saurashtra (Land of a Hundred Kingdoms), a flat peninsula stretching to the sea. Until independence, some two hundred separate kingdoms held sway here, and violence and nonviolence have been intertwined throughout the region's history. The nonviolent Jains built trading networks, and they erected beautiful white temple complexes on lofty hilltops at Palitana and Mt. Girnar. Like most traders, they depended on others to defend them. The forces of the local maharajas provided that service.

A thousand years ago on Saurashtra's shore stood the Somnath Temple, one of the world's wealthiest institutions, protected inside a walled town. Dedicated to Lord Shiva, the temple is said to have employed three hundred musicians, five hundred dancing girls, and even three hundred barbers to shave the heads of devout pilgrims. The revenues of ten thousand villages were devoted to the temple. The pillars of the shrine were studded with jewels, and images of pure gold were displayed. A massive stone lingam, representing Shiva, was worshipped daily by a thousand Brahman priests.

The lure of all this wealth was too much for Mahmud of Ghazni, predacious ruler of an Afghan territory. Every year he and his men made plundering raids into India, and Somnath was on their list. In 1030, after a vicious attack, Mahmud took the holy shrine. He and his men made off with the treasures, leaving only ruins and memories behind. Since then, Somnath has been sacked and rebuilt many times, and now an impressively beautiful new temple stands majestically on the ancient seaside site.

Near Somnath is yet another shrine to Shiva, this one far more modest. At the foot of Mt. Girnar, sacred to Jains, is a small Hindu Shiva temple where thousands of fairgoers gather each year to worship and enjoy a holiday. Country folk clad in handwoven shawls, embroidered waistcoats, glittering skirts, and tooled silver jewelry join with scores of naked sadhus—who are emulating Shiva's austerities–in the adoration of the Lord. At midnight on February's full moon night, the ash–clad sadhus march in procession to bathe in the tiny tank of the Shiva temple. In the spirit of the occasion, some of the naked holy men dance unabashedly before thousands of village spectators.

North, along Saurashtra's coast, is Dwarka, said to have been established by Lord Krishna five thousand years ago. At Dwarka's ornate ancient temple, pilgrims sing hymns to their lord, as have unnumbered generations before them.

Another special feature of the Saurashtra region is the Gir Forest, where the last of the wild Indian lions roam. Similar to the African lion, the Indian lion has a slightly smaller mane. Once widespread across northern India, the lion was the emblem of Emperor Ashoka and is now the emblem of India. Vigorously protected at the Gir National Park, the lion population there is thought to be above two hundred. Unlike African lions, Indian lions tend to get along with people without incurring too much hostility. Small homesteads of tribespeople are set within the Gir Forest, and only thorn hedges keep people and predators apart.

Much of northern Gujarat is the dry Rann of Kutch—hot, saline, flat, and very sparsely populated. Bhuj, the main town, boasts a fancy nineteenth–century palace. But more interesting are the villages in the surrounding region, where mud–walled houses are embellished inside with elaborate mud–work designs inset with flashing mirrors. The village women are expert at embroidery and create exquisite garments, quilts, and wall hangings. Their mirror–work embroidery is sold all over India, and indeed, throughout the world.

Arches and domes adorn an ornate palace of the ruler of Baroda, and an abundance of memorabilia fills its staterooms. In 1753, a Hindu warrior of Maratha descent took over the region, and his descendants ruled until Indian independence.

Madhya Pradesh: Center of Tradition

Madhya Pradesh (literally, Middle Province) sprawls across 171,000 square miles of central India. Geographically the largest state in the country, it was created in 1956 out of several geographical, cultural, and political units. Hindi is its main language, but a number of other tongues are spoken.

In this huge province of fertile farmlands sprinkled with a few cities, several natural and cultural treasures stand out. The region's long and convoluted history is revealed in the remarkable remains of prehistoric cave paintings, the Buddhist site of Sanchi, the enthralling carved temples of Khajuraho, the grand forts of Gwalior and Raisen, the palaces at Mandu, the glittering Glass Temple of Indore, as well as the enchanting tribal region of Bastar and the serene game preserve of Kanha. In many ways, perhaps, Madhya Pradesh's greatest treasure is the traditional culture kept vital in the hearts and lives of the villagers in this largely rural state.

The fertile farmland of Madhya Pradesh feeds millions of people. Small agricultural villages dot much of this state, India's largest. Here the rich fields of the Malwa Plateau stretch out to meet the Vindhyan Hills.

Colorfully dressed villagers stand before the Somnath Temple, the latest in a succession of scores of generations of reverent visitors to this sacred site.

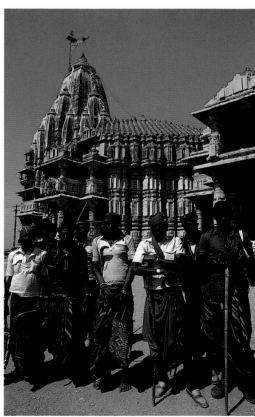

At Ahmedabad, an antique stepwell shelters a valued source of water. Sculptured stairways lead several stories underground. Stepwells are a unique feature of Gujarat's traditional architecture.

The dome and minarets of the Taj–ul–Masajid mosque dominate Bhopal's skyline. Construction was begun many decades ago by order of a Muslim queen of Bhopal, and the mosque, one of India's largest, is only now being completed.

Bhopal and Gwalior

The state's capital city is Bhopal, which before independence was the sleepy center of a princely state ruled by a series of Muslim queens. These queens (known as begams) left a legacy of honest government and a sense of valued Islamic tradition. The minarets of mosques dominate Bhopal's skyline, and in the lanes of the old city, women in black veils walk together to shops selling antique–style Bhopali wedding clothes finely embroidered in silver and gold thread.

But in Bhopal today, horse–drawn tongas have given way to roaring autorickshaws, buses, and trucks, and glossy, modern hotels are rising beside the shores of the city's lakes. Whole new industrial and residential sections have sprung up, barely mindful of Bhopal's unfortunate worldwide fame as the site of the world's largest industrial accident. In the middle of a December night in 1984, poisonous gas leaking from the Union Carbide plant left thousands dead and injured. Relief measures have yet to be fully implemented. The disaster seems almost to have inspired the city to further growth.

In the far north of the state is Gwalior, another burgeoning urban center. The famous Gwalior Fort, which the Mughal Babur dubbed "the pearl in the necklace of Indian forts," dates its beginnings to as early as the sixth century. Over the centuries, rulers and conquerors added to the great structure, which is decorated with screens, mosaics, and ornate battlements, including exterior designs of azure tiles. Here the Rani of Jhansi made her valiant last stand against the British in 1857.

The grand fort of Gwalior was the scene of fierce fighting in 1857 between the British and the Indians attempting to throw off their rule. The Rani of Jhansi made her last stand here at this ancient site.

Sandstone arches soar over the prayer hall of Bhopal's largest mosque. The stone was quarried nearby.

This Hindu holy man is a unique fixture of Bhopal. Once a military officer, he long ago chose to give up worldly attachments and live without clothing in a small shed in a city park. His only companion is a tame deer.

Bhopal is now a rapidly growing cosmopolitan city, but members of orthodox old Muslim families still follow traditional patterns of women's modesty. These young women students wear the burka veil when outside their homes.

Within the privacy of her family courtyard in Bhopal, a young Muslim woman glitters with jewelry of gold and pearls and a silk chiffon sari bordered in gold.

Ancient Stones and Traditions

Much of Madhya Pradesh's history is written in stone: the state is rich in stone, and quarrying is a big business. Stone Age hunters and gatherers have left us reminders of their presence thousands of years ago. Vivid paintings of animals, hunters, and shamans adorn rock shelters throughout the hilly center of the state. Not far from these shallow caves dwell tribal peoples who still decorate their forest huts with paintings executed in a similar style.

At Sanchi, some thirty miles east of Bhopal and six miles west of the town of Vidisha, Buddhist culture of two thousand years ago is documented in surprisingly well–preserved carvings. During the reign of the Emperor Ashoka, a great complex of Buddhist monuments and monasteries was built at Sanchi. These structures are today the finest surviving relics of the Mauryan period and are the most perfect examples of Buddhist architecture in India. Sanchi's importance synchronized with the rise and decline of Buddhism in India, between the third century and the eleventh century A.D.

When Ashoka was viceroy and heir–apparent, he visited Vidisha, and there married the daughter of a local banker, by whom he had three children. Later, atop the 275–foot high hill of Sanchi, Ashoka erected a monolithic pillar and a stupa, a dome–shaped monument covering relics of Gautama Buddha, as well as other structures. Sanchi flowered over the succeeding centuries as a center of Buddhism. Ashoka's son is reputed to have traveled as a missionary to Sri Lanka, where Buddhism flourishes today.

From the thirteenth century onward, Sanchi lay overgrown and unnoticed, until 1818, when a British general chanced upon the ruins. Years of bungled excavations and treasure–hunting followed, until finally the British government, succeeded by the Indian government, worked to carefully preserve the site and its incomparable treasures.

The great Stupa at Sanchi is the finest surviving relic of the Mauryan period of ancient Indian history and is a world-famed buddhist monument. Its finely carved gateways depict Buddhist legends and lifeways of two thousand years ago.

A country fair goes on within the shadow of the Raisen Fort, a few miles from Sanchi. Rajputs and Muslims fought long battles here. Today the ruined fort towers over a region rich in agriculture and tradition.

In the quiet of the countryside, the shrine of a village Mother Goddess is softly lit by the rising sun. Her earthen shrine may seem unassuming, but the goddess is believed to have the power of life and death over her village worshippers.

As part of the Divali festival, village cattle are fed special treats in recognition of their essential place in the village economy. In the morning, drums beat, and the cattle are assembled to be taken out for grazing.

The Great Sanchi Stupa is fifty–four feet high, surrounded by a stone railing and framed by four elaborately carved gateways (toranas). The gateway carvings depict tales of the Buddha's incarnations, life, and miracles, as well as the activities of his worshippers and representations of animals, plants, and forest spirits. The compact site includes the remains of smaller stupas, the Ashoka Pillar, monasteries, and small temples. Pilgrims from Sri Lanka and other Buddhist lands are among the many visitors to this delightful locale.

Not far from serene Sanchi is the hilltop Raisen Fort, towering five hundred feet over the small market town of Raisen. Originally constructed by Hindus, the fort was a stronghold of the fifteenth–century Sultans of Malwa. It later fell under Hindu control, and one Rajput ruler is said to have enjoyed the performances of four bands of dancing girls whose clothes were all of gold brocade.

Sowing wheat at sunset, a couple walk behind their bullock–drawn plow. In much of India, bullocks are considered the most reliable and economical source of power for plowing.

During the sixteenth century, Rajputs, Gujarati Muslims, and Afghans fought long and bloody battles here, and in 1532, seven hundred Rajput women committed jauhar rather than submit to Muslim conquerors.

Today, the fort lies deserted, but for a tiny hamlet of residents. Every Sunday, villagers gather below to make sales and purchases of grain, vegetables, clothing, and other essentials of country life. An annual fair celebrating Lord Ram's victory over the evil king Ravana draws thousands of villagers, who arrive in bullock carts and tractor–pulled trailers.

Ancient traditions are a valued part of life in the surrounding villages. Religious initiations and weddings are celebrated according to Sanskrit texts, and Hindu deities are worshipped in fire ceremonies reminiscent of the ancient Vedic rituals. Whitewashed village homes are decorated with mud bas–reliefs and inside, with small household shrines honoring gods and goddesses. The villagers work long hours sowing, cultivating, and reaping their abundant crops from fertile fields, and they mark the progress of the agricultural year with enthusiastic festival celebrations.

If Emperor Ashoka were to visit this area again, he might be startled at the sight of tractors and harvester–combines, but he would be comfortable with the vision of rustic folk walking behind their bullock–drawn plows and bending gracefully with sickles in their hands as they harvest fields of golden grain.

In western Madhya Pradesh, Ujjain and Indore are key cities. Ujjain has been a sacred city since before Buddha was born, and a number of lovely temples adorn the area. Every twelve years Ujjain is the site of the Kumbh Mela, when millions of Hindu devotees congregate to take their spiritually cleansing baths. This huge gathering is held every three years, rotating among the four cities of Ujjain, Allahabad, Hardwar, and Nasik.

Indore is not a pilgrimage center but a cotton and textile town, noted for the eighteenth–century enlightened rule of Queen Ahilya Bai. More recently, the city was the home of the late Colonel C.K. Nayudu, in his time India's premier cricketer. Indore's most famous house of worship, the Jain Glass Temple, glitters with mosaics of glass, mother–of–pearl, and colored beads. Crystal chandeliers and embossed silver reflect shimmering light.

South of Indore is the lofty site of Mandu, originally the capital of the Hindu Paramar

A Brahman father and son join in the worship of Lakshmi, the Goddess of Wealth, hoping that she will bring prosperity to their village home. To celebrate the Hindu festival of Divali, oil lamps are lit before the image of the goddess.

A few pilgrims bathe at dawn in the waters of the holy Narmada River, believed to be a goddess. The river courses through much of central India, watering both farmlands and forests. New dam projects threaten the ecological stability of the vast Narmada Valley.

Ancient traditions are valued in rural Madhya Pradesh. Here, at a wedding, women relatives of the young bride douse the groom's menfolk with colored dye, in playful joking meant to defuse tensions between the groups of in-laws.

Women peruse their prayer book at the Jain Glass Temple in Indore. Mosaics of mirrors, glass, and mother-of-pearl cover virtually every inch of wall and floor space in this dazzling house of worship.

A young village mother cradles her sleeping baby in her lap, secure in the knowledge that family traditions in India's heartland will bring her child the same satisfying sense of identity she has known.

Peaked piles of colored powders are for sale at an Indore shop. Other items for use in Hindu rituals, such as chunks of fragrant sandalwood and sweet-smelling incense sticks, are also available here.

rulers of the Malwa region. Two thousand feet high in the Vindhyan hills, the fabled city of Mandu echoed with Hindu love songs, and later, under the Sultans of Malwa, with Muslim devotions. Lovely palaces, baths, and mosques are enclosed within massive walls forty–five miles in circumference. Lakes reflect the same moon viewed by Princess Rupmati from her graceful pavilion centuries ago.

Cutting through Madhya Pradesh from east to west is the great flow of the Narmada River, worshipped as a goddess by the devout Hindu pilgrims who bathe in her sacred waters. The Narmada Valley is one of the most fertile regions of India, rich in both farmland and forests. The ecological integrity of the region is severely threatened by planned dam projects which would flood enormous areas, killing forests and displacing tribal people and wildlife.

The forests of Madhya Pradesh are peopled with tribal folk maintaining unique traditions. The Gonds once dominated much of central India and today live largely interspersed with other rural people. In the southeastern district of Bastar, Murias, Marias, and members of other groups speak their own languages and worship their own deities. Young men don bison–horn headdresses for their ceremonies. Young women in short saris wrapped above the knee join together arm in arm for their lively dances, symbolizing group harmony. In sharp contrast to the more puritan practices of the rest of India, Muria tribal teenagers enjoy each other's company in socially sanctioned dormitories. Boys present handcrafted ornamental combs to girls as tokens of affection. Unfortunately, the lure of mineral and forest resources is attracting outsiders to Bastar, and tribal lands and traditions are under severe threat.

Glimpses of Madhya Pradesh's wildlife can be seen at Kanha National Park. Here, among forested hills, roam tigers, spotted deer, swamp deer, bisonlike gaur, blackbuck, leopards, peacocks, and a great many other mammals and birds. Visitors ride out in jeeps or on elephant back to experience a taste of India as it might have been before the growth of civilization took over the land.

Young women of the Hill Maria tribal group shop for ribbons and beads at a country fair in the Bastar District of Madhya Pradesh. The people of this remote region follow unique lifeways now being threatened by outsiders.

Markets in Madhya Pradesh supply foodstuffs to many parts of the country. Golden turmeric—a key ingredient in Indian cuisine and ritual—grows abundantly here.

The tiger is still king at Kanha National Park, where wildlife is strictly protected. Visitors on elephant back are often fortunate enough to sight the elusive cats in this wooded preserve.

A cheetal, or spotted deer, stands amid greenery in Madhya Pradesh. Abundant wildlife once roamed every part of the state, but hunting and the clearing of forests have diminished wildlife populations in this rapidly developing area.

In central Madhya Pradesh, village women laboriously remove weeds from a rice plot. The work of both men and women is essential to agriculture and family prosperity.

Glorious Khajuraho

The glorious temples of Khajuraho are Madhya Pradesh's most famous attraction. Many miles from big cities or other important destinations, the village of Khajuraho draws only diligent travelers. What rewards await those who make the journey! There, amid green lawns and brilliant pink blossoms, stand twenty–two temples, glowing with the warmth of sandstone and ornamented with the sinuous curves of sculpture unparalleled anywhere else on earth.

A thousand years ago, Chandella Rajputs ruled a prosperous realm in this region, known as Bundelkhand. The founders of this dynasty are believed to have been Gond chieftains elevated to Rajput status. The court became a center of literature, art, music, and dance, and revenues raised from the reasonably content populace were devoted to the creation of exquisite temples. These temples celebrated a Hindu faith exuberant in its love of the divine. All life was seen as expressive of the divine, even human love. Union between man and woman was recognized as a culminating act of devotion, symbolic of the union of the worshipper with divine power.

The Khajuraho temples were built between approximately A.D. 900 and 1050, after the Chandellas had been in power for some time. The happy idealism they expressed was severely challenged by invaders determined to stamp out "idolatry"—and to enjoy the fruits of plunder. Soon after 1200, this area fell under Muslim domination, but the remoteness of Khajuraho apparently preserved the temples from destruction.

The surviving Khajuraho temples are considered elegant examples of the North Indian style of architecture. The heart of the temple is the "womb chamber," a dark sanctum sheltering the symbol of the deity, surrounded by antechambers and halls, and surmounted by a soaring spire with rounded top.

The grandest temple at Khajuraho is the Kandariya Mahadev Temple, dedicated to Shiva. The inner sanctum contains a lingam four feet around. Above a lofty terrace, halls and pavilions are crowned with domed spires pushing upward like a succession of foothills approaching a mountainous main tower, symbolizing the lofty Himalayan peaks where the gods are said to dwell.

The entrance archway is adorned with sculptures—scrolls, scallops, beasts, dwarfs, flowers, and flying deities. The outside is decorated with bands of sculpture that leave the viewer astonished: Hindu gods and goddesses, curvaceous celestial maidens, and human couples engaged in acts of love and erotic union. Here, sensual delight is clearly celebrated.

The other temples of Khajuraho display a wealth of sculptural beauty, evoking the grandeur of the snow–capped Himalayas and the earthy pleasures of life. A few of the smaller structures are Jain, with austerely posed deities.

Looking at these awe–inspiring temples, one can glimpse a complex and beautiful way of looking at the world and God, and perhaps gain an expanded understanding of the human experience.

Maharashtra: Precious Past and Powerful Present

The state of Maharashtra (literally, Great Country) combines the surging energy of modern Bombay with the scenic grandeur of the Western Ghat hill chain and the incomparable carved cave temples of centuries long past. Although Bombay is home to many immigrants from other parts of the nation, and many Maharashtrians belong to gentle priestly and artisan traditions, a great number of Maharashtrians proudly claim ties to the militant Marathas who staunchly defended this land from foreign conquerors.

The wondrous temples of Khajuraho are famed for the glory of their fine sculptures. The grandest structure at Khajuraho is the Kandariya Mahadev Temple, its spires rising skyward in praise of Lord Shiva.

At Khajuraho, loving couples move together in eternal harmony. Here, Lakshmi, the Goddess of Fortune, is embraced by her eternal consort, Lord Vishnu. Lakshmi is considered feminine beauty personified.

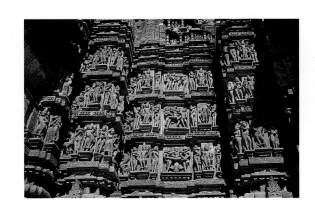

The temple sculptures celebrate life and love with captivating imagery. The importance of life–generating union between male and female is aesthetically evoked.

The Gateway of India, Bombay's celebrated waterfront landmark, was built in 1924 to commemorate the 1911 visit of King George V to India. Facing this memorial to the British Raj is a statue of Shivaji, the great seventeenth—century Maratha leader.

Members of the Parsi community add a special leavening to Bombay's mix. Originally from Persia, they worship sacred fire at their temples with gates guarded by pre—Islamic figures. Many of India's most successful business people are Parsis.

Tankers line up in Bombay's busy harbor, led by the Netaji Subhas Bose, named for a famed Bengali revolutionary. As the prime port for the world's second most populous nation, Bombay is constantly bustling.

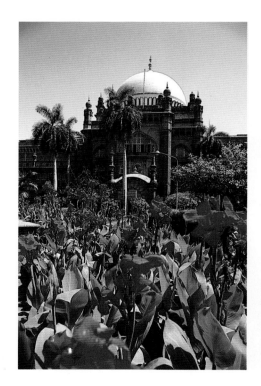

Brilliant blossoms blaze with color in the gardens of the Prince of Wales Museum, a treasurehouse of Indian art. The museum was built in honor of King George V's first visit to India in 1905, when he was still the Prince of Wales.

Commuters cram into local trains, carrying them to and fro between outlying suburbs and the crowded peninsula of downtown Bombay. Industriousness and constant activity are hallmarks of Bombay life.

Energetic Bombay

Bombay, India's economic powerhouse, pulses with power and energy. The streets and rails are busy with purposeful traffic—cars, taxis, red buses, trucks, commuter trains, and crowds of people—office workers, business workers, shoppers, laborers, merchants, all moving rapidly in the quest of finishing a job and getting on with the future. The harbor waters, too, are active with ships from all over the world, loading and unloading cargo, with launches and dhows, and all sorts of boats plying to and fro. There is a tremendous spirit of zest and vitality in Bombay.

This great city of more than ten million people is the capital of the state of Maharashtra and also the commercial capital of the whole country. Center of industry, transportation, and communications, its fine harbor on the Arabian Sea makes it one of the world's busiest ports.

Bombay is very important in manufacturing, especially in textiles. At least one–third of the cloth needed to clothe a nation of 860 million people is produced here. Goods manufactured elsewhere are often trans–shipped through the city's port and railway and trucking centers.

The city is also a center of culture and intellectual activity. Gateway to the nation, Bombay welcomes the world's material and cultural offerings into India. Educational institutions are numerous and active. Bombay is the nerve center of India's film industry, the largest in the world. Hundreds of films are produced here each year.

Bombay is crowded—its people are packed into a funnel–shaped peninsula, with major housing shortages; nevertheless, five hundred new residents arrive every day, drawn by the promise of opportunity. Bombay municipal authorities are working as fast as they can to fill in channels and wetlands, creating more ground for building, but they cannot work fast enough to meet the demand for space. Luxury

A relaxed merchant awaits customers at his cloth shop. Purchased goods will be wrapped in pieces of recycled newspaper or printed notices, hanging on a nearby hook. In India, virtually nothing goes to waste.

Bombay's clothes are washed at the Dhobi Ghats—a huge facility for hand–laundering by members of the Dhobi (Washerman) caste. After being line–dried, clothes are pressed and carefully returned to their owners.

Devout Catholics attend mass at a Bombay church. Christianity is a popular faith in some areas of India, particularly where Portuguese and British influence were strong.

and middle–income housing units are rising fast, but millions are jammed into inadequate tenements and slums.

In many ways—especially in its energy and geography—Bombay is like New York. Its island location, on the coast, with rivers between it and the mainland, is the source of much of its success—and of its problems.

Bombay was once a sleepy fishing village on a quiet coastline. The Portuguese took it over in 1534, and it became part of the dowry Catherine of Braganza brought to her marriage with England's Charles II in 1661. The British recognized the value of Bombay's natural harbor and encouraged its development. They were greatly aided by the industrious Parsis—Persian Zoroastrians who had settled in Gujarat and moved to Bombay in 1670. Parsi entrepreneurial spirit has been essential to Bombay's success.

The Civil War in the United States also gave the new port a big boost. As supplies of American cotton shriveled, Bombay's young cotton and textile mills received many orders. In 1862, a major land reclamation project united the area's original seven

Bombay's Crawford Market offers a potpourri of fresh produce and other goods under a roof providing welcome shelter from the tropical sun. Little–noticed bas–reliefs at the market were designed by Rudyard Kipling's father.

Trains from all over India rumble into Victoria Terminus, Bombay's ornate railway station, built in 1888. Bombay is the commercial center of India and welcomes a constant flow of visitors and migrants.

Ganesh is honored throughout India, but his birthday celebrations are especially grand in Bombay. Elaborate images are paraded through the streets and then ritually immersed in the ocean. The festival gives Bombay-ites a sense of community in the midst of the huge metropolis.

Players vigorously attack the ball in a game of field hockey. In cities like Bombay, field hockey is a popular sport.

islands, and the city began to expand dramatically.

There is great diversity here. People of every religion call Bombay home, and schools are taught in twelve languages, even though Marathi is the most common language of the region. English is spoken everywhere in the city. Economically, people range from multimillionaire capitalists to middle–class administrators on down to the lowest economic stratum of pavement–dwelling laborers. Bombay people tend to be very active politically.

In addition to their vigorous secular lives, Bombayites keep their traditions alive. They participate in a great city–wide Hindu festival, Ganesh Chaturthi, celebrating the birthday of the auspicious, elephant–headed God of Good Fortune, and expressing a sense of unity for many of Bombay's people.

Bombay continues to grow in energy and vitality, a magnet for millions seeking better lives. It is a marvelously complex and fascinating place.

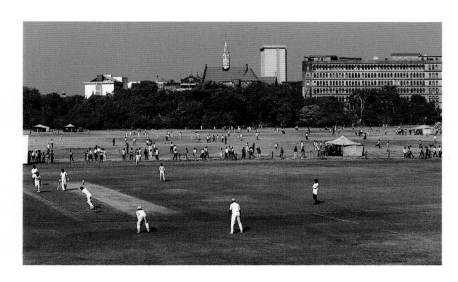

A vividly colored statue of Ganesh, the Hindu God of Good Fortune, is worshipped on the occasion of Ganesh Chaturthi, the god's birthday.

Some British traditions still flourish on Indian soil. Cricket is an extremely popular sport. Here players enjoy a game at the Bombay Gymkhana Club.

At the Elephanta Caves, a monumental image of Lord Shiva is lit with the glow of a single votive lamp, reverently offered by a worshipper. Garlands of fresh flowers adorn the mystical figure, carved from solid rock more than fourteen hundred years ago.

In some of Ajanta's caves, paintings still tell ancient tales. Courtly life and love as well as hundreds of Buddhist legends and stories provide motifs for a multitude of remarkably well–preserved murals.

During the second century B.C., monks and artisans began the labor of centuries, ultimately carving twenty–nine elaborate caves from the rock cliff of Ajanta. They created one of the greatest remaining monuments of the ancient world.

Elephanta

An hour's trip by launch across Bombay's blue harbor takes one to green Elephanta Island, a place to ponder the precious past. Here, almost within sight of the nuclear energy plant at Trombay, one can go back in time almost fifteen hundred years. At Elephanta, a set of caves provides an introduction to Maharashtra's finest offerings—exquisitely carved cave temples. Although some of the carvings were badly damaged by Portuguese soldiers, Elephanta provides the hors d'oeuvre before the main repast of Ajanta and Ellora.

After practicing for a few centuries at other locations, honing their skills from generation to generation, western India's most expert stone carvers came to Elephanta in about the mid-sixth century. They climbed a tall hill and carefully selected a rock formation upon which to work. Excavating and carving from the top down, so no scaffolding was ever needed, they created a symphony in stone in praise of Lord Shiva. The main cave is a grand, pillared chamber adorned with large, powerful sculptures of Shiva in his many aspects. The cave walls are otherwise plain, enhancing the impact of the images.

The central focus is a twenty–foot–high bust of Lord Shiva in three–headed form, symbolizing his fierce, feminine, and meditative qualities. In the gloom of the cave, with just a modicum of light illuminating the divine form, the effect is almost mystical. On Shiva's festival days, worshippers come from the city to honor the image with flower garlands and tiny devotional lamps. Other sculptures depict Shiva energetically creating the world through his cosmic dance, Shiva's marriage with Parvati, and Shiva as half–man/half–woman, signifying the essential unity of the sexes and of cosmic forces. As art historian J.C. Harle has written, the Elephanta sculptures convey the essential oneness of the human and the divine, which is the greatest theme of Indian art. The skill with which these figures communicate that essential idea has perhaps never been equaled.

Ajanta and Ellora

With aesthetic appetite whetted by Elephanta, one must move on to the carved caves of Ajanta and Ellora, ranked high among the greatest wonders of the world. Northeast of Bombay, near Aurangabad, are two astonishing series of temples carved out of the living rock over the course of fourteen centuries. After their heyday, the caves were abandoned. Ajanta was forgotten until 1819, when a British hunting party stumbled upon the site.

During the second century B.C., wandering Buddhist monks selected as a site for their meditations a semicircular forested gorge with a river flowing below. As centuries passed, great numbers of monks and artisans labored at excavating a set of twenty–nine caves, some monks' cells and monasteries, others Buddhist temples with stupas inside, all carved from the rock cliff of Ajanta. The caves are adorned with elaborate sculptures and paintings.

The sculptures are finely wrought images of animals, guards, and deities, while the paintings give us rare glimpses of what life was like for the nobility of centuries ago. Intended to instruct the monks on the temptations of the world and on what the princely Buddha had given up when he became an ascetic wanderer, the cave murals depict court life in all its pleasurable panoply. Sensuous dancers, richly caparisoned elephants, gem–ornamented princes, and buxom, thin–waisted princesses all move through the paintings, living and loving in worldly delight. Amid these beautiful images of mundane pleasures are sculptures of Buddha, calm in contemplation.

Ajanta's caves are Buddhist shrines, some completed long before others. Simple monks' cells contrast with grander excavations like this cave temple featuring a solid stone stupa beneath a vaulted ceiling carved to look as if it were supported by wooden beams, as were earlier wooden temples.

After nine centuries, in the seventh century A.D., the focus shifted to Ellora, some seventy–five miles away, where another set of caves was created from living rock. Here, not only Buddhism, but Hinduism and the Jain faith inspired the four centuries of arduous labors needed to create these elaborate excavations. The Buddhist and Jain caves are ornately carved, but are relatively calm, while the Hindu caves seem to burst with divine energy.

The most majestic creation is the Kailasa Temple, a full–sized freestanding temple flanked by huge elephants, all carved from solid rock. Pillars and podiums, towering spires and passionate deities emerged as the workers dug away some 200,000 tons of rock. The result is an awe–inspiring representation of Shiva's Himalayan abode. Nearby caves are alive with stone murals depicting divine struggles and victories. With these caves before us, it is clear that India far surpasses the rest of the world in the glory of its rock–cut architecture.

India is supreme among all nations in the splendor of its rock–cut architecture. At Ellora, Buddhist, Hindu, and Jain caves were excavated from the living rock. The awe–inspiring eighth–century Kailasa Temple at Ellora is considered the most splendid rock–cut monument in the world.

A friendly sadhu strolls the streets of Pune, one of India's largest and most forward–thinking cities. He bears the brass image of a powerful goddess upon his breast and offers blessings to those who make offerings to her.

Proud Memories

Maharashtra proudly honors the memory of the brave Maratha warriors of this region. The Marathas challenged the Mughals and the British and ruled kingdoms across western and central India. Shivaji, the great seventeenth–century Maratha leader, was raised a devout Hindu in the Deccan Plateau city of Pune (Poona), and led his troops in successful assaults on Mughal strongholds. Maratha soldiers of fortune carved out kingdoms for themselves, establishing the great states of Indore, Gwalior, Baroda, and many others.

Since then, Pune has long been a center of learning and social progress. Mahatma Gandhi and his wife Kasturba were interned here by the British, and Kasturba Gandhi died here. More recently, the late Guru Rajneesh established his ashram in Pune.

Aurangabad still rings with the pious exhortations of Emperor Aurangzeb, who made it his capital, and the medieval fort of Daulatabad displays the scars of valiantly fought battles. Nasik, a picturesque Hindu pilgrimage center, plays host to the Kumbh Mela every twelve years, when crowds of the faithful bathe in the Godavari, one of the Deccan's most sacred rivers.

Festive fun and spiritual concerns combine for huge crowds of pilgrims at the Kumbh Mela in Nasik, Maharashtra. The waters of the Godavari, one of the Deccan region's most sacred rivers, wash away sins and daily cares—at least temporarily.

Dawn breaks gloriously over the Himalayas in India's northeast. Mount Kanchenjunga, marking India's border with Nepal, is the world's third–tallest peak and presents an awesome sight from the foothills at Darjeeling.

Eastern India's emerald fields yield lush crops of rice, but only after farmers and their oxen work long hours in muddy plots. These cultivators of Assam keep watch by night in shaded sheds to protect their crops from wild animals.

The Radiant East

The sun rises in the east, its glow spreading upward from the dark horizon. Its radiant beams illuminate the high mountain peaks of eastern India with a golden glow. Growing ever brighter, the rosy rays of the rising orb light up the dewy green forests and fields of the far eastern states, signaling songbirds and slumbering rhinoceros to start their daily foraging. The sun's radiant light rushes west, striking the sleepy–eyed street dwellers of Calcutta and the temple spires of sea–washed shores. India's east is where the nation first meets each shining new day. Indeed, India's easternmost state is named Arunachal Pradesh–the Province of Dawn.

India's eastern region is a complex conglomeration of varied venues–majestic mountains, pristine forests, verdant rice fields, charming temple towns, ancient cities, and the brash metropolis of Calcutta. Tribal folk, farmers, slumlords, and saints all inhabit this fascinating area.

A look at the map brings a quick reminder that India's east is almost cut in two by Bangladesh, carved out of what once was India, then East Pakistan, to form an independent nation. Land travel between Calcutta and regions to the east almost always involves going north to pass through the sliver of land linking the main body of Indian territory with the easternmost seven states.

Orissa: Territory of Temples

Emerald fields of rice shaded by palm trees, beautiful beaches of crystal sand, clusters of exquisite antique temples, monsoon woodland waterfalls, and spectacularly colorful festivals: this is Orissa, a large state covering much of India's eastern shore along the Bay of Bengal. This predominantly agricultural region was once the site of the great kingdom of Kalinga, and voyagers out from ancient Orissa brought Hindu culture to ports in Southeast Asia. The word "rice" is thought to be derived from Orissa's name.

Orissa's convoluted history is revealed in the stones of thousands of temples dotting the land. Some temples are in ruins, while others remain dynamic centers of Hinduism. To witness the great festival of Lord Jagannath at his temple in Puri is to be part of an event that has been going on for a thousand years or more. Visiting Orissa's villages is to experience a sense of what life may have been like centuries ago.

Emperor Ashoka was determined to conquer ancient Kalinga, and his armies won a bloody battle there. It is said that Ashoka was so horrified at what he had wrought that he repented his misdeeds and adopted the nonviolent faith of Buddhism, at that time the religion of Orissa. He left rock edicts still visible near the once–bloody battlefields of the third century B.C., now serene paddy fields. Later, another ruler brought Jainism into the ascendant, but Jainism was replaced by the return of Buddhism in about A.D. 100.

The height of Orissan civilization was reached between the fourth and thirteenth centuries, when Hindu kings of the Kesari and Ganga dynasties ruled the land. The great temples of Lingaraj at Bhubaneswar, of Jagannath at Puri, and of the Sun at Konarak were built during these brilliant periods.

Afghans and Mughals came through in the sixteenth century, and the Dutch arrived to see what might interest them. The Marathas controlled the region for a while, but then the British took over in 1803. Since Indian independence, efforts have been made to expand irrigation as well as industry and high–tech companies, but the state retains a pleasant rural atmosphere.

About a quarter of the state's population belong to some sixty–two tribal groups whose ancestors lived in Orissa long before the Aryans

Virile dancers from Orissa brandish swords in the Republic Day parade in the nation's capital. Orissa's convoluted history has shaped a province rich in regional tradition.

invaded India. Having been pushed back to hilly and forested areas, they have managed to retain much of their traditional culture, although outside influences are bringing change. The Bondos are particularly striking, since the women wear very short wrapped skirts and many heavy necklaces, and often shave their heads. The tribal areas of Orissa are just across the state border from those of Madhya Pradesh.

Bhubaneswar

Bhubaneswar, the state capital, is known as the City of Temples because at one time some seven thousand temples adorned the town. Today a mere five hundred remain, including the Lingaraj Temple, one of India's greatest houses of worship. Although non–Hindus may not enter, they can scan the temple compound from a viewing platform originally erected for Lord Curzon during the days of the British Raj.

Dedicated to Lord Shiva, the temple follows the northern Indian style of architecture, with a large central spire surrounded by lesser spires. The intricately carved Lingaraj tower rises 150 feet to the sky, proclaiming the glory of the Lord of Three Worlds. Most of the temple dates from about A.D. 1000, but parts are over fourteen hundred years old. The temple walls enclose more than fifty smaller temples and shrines.

Close to Bhubaneshwar are clusters of small temples, among which the small Mukteswar and Raj Rani Temples are especially fine. The temples are covered with intricately carved female warriors, erotic scenes, elephants, monkeys, dwarfs, and nymphs. Not far away is a set of charming carved caves, including one that must be entered through the mouth of a carved beast.

Puri and Divine Chariots

It is at Puri that the deep faith of Orissa's Hindus is most evident. Puri is one of Hinduism's most important pilgrimage destinations, and travelers come here from all over the country to bathe in the sacred surging ocean surf. But the prime object of the pilgrims' devotion is the Lord of the World, Jagannath. His grand temple tower is 175 feet tall, visible from afar. Inside the huge temple compound, which non–Hindus cannot enter, many thousands of temple servants wait upon the Lord and his worshippers, carrying out elaborate rituals. Until recent decades, some women pledged their lives to the Lord, honoring him with their performances of sensuous dances of great antiquity.

A deity with possibly very ancient origins, Jagannath is regarded as a reincarnation of Vishnu. Together with his brother and his sister, Jagannath is represented by a brightly painted wooden image with large round eyes. Every twelve or nineteen years (depending on the permutations of the Hindu lunar–solar calendar), the crude images are replaced with new icons hewn from sanctified logs. In a dramatic midnight ritual, a blindfolded hereditary woodcarver opens the chest cavities of the old images and takes from each a small casket bearing the "life force" of the image. The caskets are placed within the new images, and the holes plugged up. The carver's hands are wrapped in cloth, and he may neither see nor touch these sacred items. No one knows what is inside the caskets. The old images, now "dead," are buried, and the new images brought forth for worship. Continuity with untold scores of past generations is maintained today through these sacred rites.

Every June or July, Lord Jagannath and his siblings are taken out on a week–long sacred journey to a temple about a mile away. The holy images ride in huge carts—with their tall colorful peaks, these resemble the Jagganath Temple itself. The festival is known as the Rath Yatra, or Journey of the Carts,

A mask of carved wood vividly represents the face of a goddess. Such masks are worn in Puri street dramas in celebration of annual festivals. Male performers enthusiastically enact mythological themes.

The tower of Lord Jagannath's temple at Puri reaches 175 feet into the sky behind colorful temple carts. Thousands of devotees will join in pulling the sacred vehicles forward during the Rath Yatra festival.

Jagannath, Lord of the World, a reincarnation of Vishnu, rules at Puri, where his great Rath Yatra festival is celebrated each June or July. Carts resembling moving temples are readied to convey him and his brother and sister on a divine journey.

The great Lingaraj Temple at Bhubaneswar is one of India's most eminent houses of worship. Hindus throng here from all over the country to pay their respects to Lord Shiva at this ancient edifice topped by a 150–foot–high tower.

Creating a cosmic chariot for the Sun God was the task of twelve hundred artisans seven hundred years ago at Konarak. Unfortunately, the great central tower of the Sun Temple fell before it was completed.

Huge wheels of stone seem ready to move Konarak's celestial coach forward to a divine destination. Intricate carvings of loving couples provide glimpses of more earthly pleasures.

The fierce Goddess Kali guards her namesake city. Crowded Calcutta takes its name from Kali Ghat, where the powerful feminine force is offered goat sacrifices. This colorful clay image was fashioned for a festival.

and it is from this event that the English word "juggernaut" derives. Led by the former Maharaja of Puri, hundreds of thousands of people gather to help pull the carts, sure that their devoted service will bring rewards in the afterlife. In past centuries, ecstatic devotees sometimes threw themselves under the huge wheels of the divine chariots. The spectacle of the Cart Festival is quite stupendous, vivid proof of the vitality of ancient Hindu traditions.

Near Puri is the quiet town of Konarak, site of the famous Sun Temple, erected around A.D. 1250 by twelve hundred artisans working steadily for sixteen years. The architect's concept was that of a colossal stone replica of the Sun God's cosmic chariot. Huge wheels bracket the base of the temple, and a team of carved horses at the front seems to provide the enormous structure with the means to move forward. Gravity, however, dictated that the central tower of the temple would fall even before it was completed. Still, this unique edifice, adorned with erotic sculptures and representations of musicians, curving vines and flowers, animals, and courtesans, presents a fascinating picture of the past.

After visiting these temples, so much the products of fervor and exertion, a quiet walk on the beach is quite soothing. With the silken waves of the Bay of Bengal lapping at one's feet, the visitor can watch lithe fishermen launch their wooden boats into the dawn–lit waters much as their ancestors did hundreds of years ago.

West Bengal: Gift of the River

As the great River Ganga flows across northern India, it is joined by many tributaries, all surging with water and silt gathered from all across the land. As the Ganga approaches the sea, it is joined by the mighty Brahmaputra River, carrying its own silty gifts. The mighty flows deposit their silt, building the great delta of the Ganga. Here on this fertile, low–lying flat land is West Bengal, with Bangladesh close at hand. Verdant fields are watered by the many branches of the river—excessively watered during heavy monsoons and cyclones. But the land has proven fruitful enough to support an abundant population.

West Bengal—which then, with Bangladesh, was part of the larger region of Bengal—was the pride of the British empire. The British adventurer Robert Clive had wrested the area from the hands of its Muslim ruler, Nawab Siraj–ud–Daula, at the 1757 Battle of Plassey. The riches that Bengal produced gladdened the hearts of fortune–seeking foreigners, not to mention monarchs, for quite some time. The Bengali people produced many major thinkers and political activists, always challenging the British. Since independence in 1947 and the creation of the state of West Bengal, intellectual and political vibrancy have continued to enliven the region.

Calcutta: Life at its Most Intense

The maelstrom of the metropolis of Calcutta is almost beyond description. More than eleven million people live, love, laugh, and labor in this urban center, the largest in India, and fourth largest in the world. The streets and avenues of the city are jammed with people going about their business, striving to meet their occupational goals, trying to provide for their families and attempting to get through life with a reasonable degree of satisfaction. For all but the most privileged, achieving these aims can be very challenging. The city's services and infrastructure are inadequate to the task of meeting the needs of so many people, and nature, in the form of heat and floods, can play havoc with human plans. Still, the people of Calcutta are uniquely vibrant, always celebrating life with a poem or a festival, enjoying the delights that simply being alive can bring.

Three hundred years ago, at the very end of the seventeenth century, an agent for the British East India Company purchased three quiet villages for a British settlement that would become Calcutta. The British set up a small fort, which the local Muslim ruler attacked, leading to the legendary incident of the Black Hole of Calcutta. British prisoners were jammed into a small chamber, resulting in their demise. Robert Clive came marching in, and from that time forward, the British were a force to be reckoned with in the area.

Calcutta developed apace, becoming a prosperous commercial center and capital of British India. Trade burgeoned in cotton, silk, lacquer, indigo, rice, tobacco, tea, and jute. Fancy monuments were built alongside fashionable boulevards, and a great open space, the Maidan, provided refreshing breathing room. In 1911, the capital of the Raj was moved to Delhi. World War II and the partition of Bengal severely constricted trade–the jute mills of Calcutta were cut off from their Bangladesh source of raw fiber. Further, synthetic fibers reduced worldwide demand for jute. Refugees came

Traffic at this Calcutta corner runs smoothly, a rarity in this bursting city. Many intersections are jammed with vehicles, pedestrians, and animals, all busily trying to cope with living in one of the world's most rapidly growing metropolises.

The Victoria Memorial reflects colonial power in Calcutta, once the capital and most profitable center of British rule in India. The monument dates from the early twentieth century and is today a museum for relics of the Raj.

The powerful Goddess Durga has many arms with which to vanquish her enemies. Demons are no match for her and the lion or tiger on which she rides. Fabulous images of the goddess are created, worshipped, paraded, and immersed in sacred water during Calcutta's great celebration of Durga Puja.

A Jain temple in Calcutta is ornamented with fanciful towers and curving arches. Glass mosaics glitter on pillars and pavilions as worshippers pay their respects to Jainism's austere saints.

pouring into the city, straining its resources well beyond capacity.

The governing forces of Calcutta and West Bengal struggle to meet the demands and legitimate needs of the populace, but the tasks are overwhelming. The elected government is Communist, sparked by plenty of debate and activism. The authorities have achieved much, helping to increase agricultural yields and literacy, even decreasing the percentage of people living below the poverty line. Still, more than 150,000 people make their homes on the pavements of Calcutta, and Mother Teresa's sisters keep busy tending to a great number of truly destitute human beings. Nonetheless, for people from the countryside, Calcutta seems to offer opportunity, and hundreds arrive here each day.

Visitors to Calcutta marvel at many sights. The Howrah Bridge across the Hooghly River is a chaotic crush of traffic of every kind–cars, scooters, bicycles, pushcarts, ox–carts, and rickshaws drawn by thin men. On the Maidan, the main building is the domed Victoria Memorial, built of white marble brought from Rajasthan. Here the Queen–Empress is immortalized among the children of the people whose labors brought so much wealth to her realm. Perhaps her regal statue enjoys the view of the constant lively activity going on at the Maidan—concerts, plays, lectures, joggers, army drills, cricket games, preaching sadhus, picnics, and political rallies.

The Calcutta Racecourse, opened in 1819, features a polo club grounds, and is a gathering place for high society. Kalighat, the site of a temple to the fierce goddess Kali, is active with worshippers bringing offerings, including sacrificial goats. Rabindra Mancha, an eighteenth–century house where the Nobel Laureate poet Rabindranath Tagore was born in 1861, is now a museum memorializing his life and thoughts.

Throughout the vibrant city, churches, bazaars, government buildings, golf clubs, rowing clubs, art academies, universities, mosques, gardens, teashops, newspaper offices, museums, prosperous residential neighborhoods, and makeshift slums all pulse with a constant parade of spirited life.

Upcountry in West Bengal

Moving south of Calcutta, one arrives in the Sundarbans, the "beautiful forest" of the very edge of the delta, where the flow of branches of the Ganga mixes with the salty waters of the sea. Travel is difficult here, and nature is hostile. The inhabitants paddle skiffs through the marshy mangrove jungle, always fearful that tigers may attack. Sundarbans tigers have no fear of humans, but prefer to attack from behind. The men who work in the area have taken to wearing masks of human faces on the backs of their heads, which has cut down the attack rate considerably. Estuarine crocodiles, the largest in the world, can also be seen lounging along the mud flats.

Traveling ninety miles north of Calcutta, one reaches Shanti Niketan (Abode of Peace), an open–air institution created in 1901 by the Nobel Prize–winning writer, philosopher, and painter Rabindranath Tagore. Tagore is credited with expanding the outside world's knowledge of the greatness of India's history and culture. Indira Gandhi was a graduate of this hub of intellectual life.

North of Shanti Niketan, the state of West Bengal narrows almost to a thread and barely expands again until its northernmost point in the foothills of the Himalayas, where Darjeeling, a delightful hill station, is situated. Here, in sharp contrast to the flat landscape of the delta, mountains dominate the landscape, and waterfalls gush down sharp ravines. Brilliant green tea plantations cover terraced slopes. The air is clear and delightful, the pace unhurried. The town is approached by a winding road, or by a tiny train which wends its way up the steep hills.

Dawn–lit mists rise above the charming hill town of Darjeeling. Far from the hot and steamy plains below, Darjeeling offers bracing air and an unhurried pace and was once the summer capital of British India.

Copper trumpets sound at Yiga–Choling Buddhist Monastery in Ghoom, a few miles outside Darjeeling. Founded a century ago, the monastery houses a huge gilded image of Maitreya (Future Buddha), reflecting the faith of many of the region's people.

During the hot season, the British government used to pack up its papers from its Calcutta offices and haul everything to Darjeeling. The town's architecture clearly shows its British origins, and the mists drifting over the hills are very reminiscent of the British Isles. Today's population is certainly not British, however—Nepalis, Lepchas, Tibetans, and Bhotiyas enliven this scenic spot. Tibetan prayer flags flutter in the breezes, and Buddhist houses of worship display colorful images of Lord Buddha.

Shrouded in mists, Darjeeling itself is beautiful enough. But there is something more. Having gone to sleep in a mist–shrouded night, one can rise at dawn, throw open the shutters, and find that the mists have parted. There, lit by the brilliance of the rising sun, is the glorious sight of the majestic snow–covered Mount Kanchenjunga. The beauty of this Himalayan peak is completely overpowering and can never be forgotten.

Darjeeling tea is tenderly plucked by workers moving slowly through cool green fields, surrounded by verdant vistas. Connoisseurs of fine tea owe much to the careful labors of the tea pluckers.

Mt. Kanchenjunga, divine home of the gods, towers above Sikkim and the surrounding region with overwhelming snow–capped beauty.

At Rumtek Monastery, west of Gangtok, Sikkim's capital, fierce deities guard heavenly and earthly spheres. The monastery was built in the 1960s as a replica of a Tibetan monastery destroyed by the Chinese.

In Sikkim, India's most highly elevated state, rice terraces are cultivated by villagers of Lepcha and Nepali descent.

Sikkim: Himalayan Kingdom

Mount Kanchenjunga and its surrounding range are actually located in Sikkim, where awe–inspiring snowcapped peaks completely dominate the landscape. The third highest mountain in the world (28,200 feet), Kanchenjunga is revered as the home of the gods. In its shadow are verdant forests nurturing wild orchids, red pandas, blossoms, birds, and butterflies. Buddhist monasteries ornament the scene, with bright paintings, sculptures, and masked festival dancers.

A few decades ago, Sikkim was featured in the news when an American woman became the bride of the Chogyal (ruler) of the mountain kingdom of Sikkim. In a Tibetan Buddhist ceremony in the capital town of Gangtok, silk scarves were exchanged while prominent society leaders from East and West looked on, and the world learned about the existence of this lovely Himalayan realm. Since then, the American has gone back to Manhattan, the Chogyal has entered a new phase of the cosmic cycle of life, and Sikkim has become an Indian state. Outsiders may enter only with a special pass issued by the Indian government.

Actually, the area has long been a zone of contention, with Tibetans, Gurkhas, English, Bhutanese, and Chinese all having designs on the tiny, but strategically located, territory. Visitors with no interest in military conquest can focus on the royal chapel and palace, which hold impressive murals, Buddhist altars, and sculptures. In the countryside, they can admire women in Tibetan–style robes paying their respects to chortens, small Buddhist shrines containing relics, and they can view terraced rice fields, carefully cultivated by Nepalese immigrants to Sikkim.

When the Chinese occupied Tibet, a lama of the Karmapa sect of Tibet took refuge in Sikkim. With the chogyal's blessing, Rumtek Monastery was created, a replica of the gompa at Chhofuk in Tibet. After his death in 1982, the lama was cremated and his sacred relics preserved in a golden reliquary at Rumtek. Many of Sikkim's monasteries are far older than Rumtek and, like Rumtek, are adorned with frescoes and statues fully expressive of the vigor of Himalayan Buddhism. Adding a spectacular backdrop to virtually every vista in Sikkim is the snow–crowned majesty of Mount Kanchenjunga.

Tibetan influences are strong in Sikkim, as at this small Buddhist monastery overlooking Himalayan peaks and valleys. Prayer flags flutter in the mountain breezes.

Assam: Meeting Ground of Nature and Many Cultures

To the east of Sikkim, south of Bhutan, is the state of Assam, its easternmost reaches pointing toward Burma. Here, cultural influences from southeast Asia are apparent, mixed with cultural patterns typical of subcontinental India. Assam has long been a zone of struggle and mixture between peoples of Aryan, Dravidian, and Southeast Asian heritages. In centuries past, Thai tribes clashed with Mughals for supremacy. The Burmese and the British vied for power, and during World War II, the Japanese coveted this strategic area as a pathway to the Indian plains.

Today, conflict continues, now between the Assamese and immigrants, especially Bengali Hindus from India and Muslims from Bangladesh, all seeking escape from poverty.

Assam is a strikingly beautiful region. The broad flow of the mighty Brahmaputra River cuts through the length of the state, watering rich rice fields. Emerald–green tea plantations abound, producing leaves for the teapots of much of the tea–drinking world. Guwahati, the state capital, boasts fine Hindu temples. Perhaps the most intriguing of these is the Kamakhya Temple atop Nichala Hill, dedicated to Shiva's wife in her form as the goddess Shakti. The hill represents Shiva's lingam, phallic emblem of cosmic power in its male manifestation, and within the temple is a moist natural stone yoni (reproductive organ), symbolic of female generative power.

A sense of primordial nature permeates Assam's game sanctuaries, Kaziranga and Manas. Both parks are home to wild elephants and the Indian rhinoceros, saved from extinction despite the predations of poachers who sell the horn to Chinese customers. (The Chinese believe the erect horn, ground up and consumed, increases sexual potency.) At Kaziranga, tall green swamp grass shelters the prehistoric–looking rhinos as they root about in the light of dawn, white birds daintily plucking insects from their rough hides. It is possible to approach these huge animals while riding on an even larger beast, an elephant–and while the rhino may threaten, it hesitates to charge the elephant.

Herds of wild elephants move about the swamps of Kaziranga, and wild and tame elephants sometimes meet to caress one another. Swamp deer, wild boar, wild buffalo, tigers, leopards, and birds of all kinds are seen here in this place out of time, where nature is supreme and man is but a privileged spectator.

Assam's temples express cultural traditions unique to the Brahmaputra region, blending influences from subcontinental India with traits from the Burmese hills

In Guwahati, Assam's small capital, an unusual temple venerates female powers of generation. Walking beneath a garlanded image of Lord Ganesh, a red–robed priest emerges from the temple's inner sanctum.

Passengers crowd aboard a ferry on the Brahmaputra River. This mighty river, known literally as Son of Brahma, cuts through the length of Assam State before turning southward to the sea.

Village women of Assam transplant delicate rice seedlings. The people of the state are almost entirely dependent upon agriculture, and there are few urban centers in the region.

Assam's forests and fields yield bamboo and grasses for building village homes. Here, banana plants and palm trees grow in a verdant garden.

The long-horned wild buffalo survives only in small pockets. Genetically related to domestic buffaloes, the most important domestic animal in Southeast Asia, wild buffalo bulls sometimes commandeer domestic buffalo cows.

An Indian rhinoceros enjoys a mud bath at Assam's Kaziranga National Park. The prehistoric—looking beasts once ranged widely over northern India's grassy floodplains but are now confined to a few parks in Assam, West Bengal, Bihar, and Nepal.

Nature's primordial cycles continue at Kaziranga Park, where an elephant tends her baby along the shore of the Brahmaputra.

Herds of as many as two hundred wild elephants can be seen in Assam's lush natural areas. Bulls tusked and tuskless test each other's mettle.

A red panda, or catbear, peers from his perch in a tree. The white–faced animals have a long bushy tail and live at high altitudes throughout the eastern Himalayan region.

Silver falls stream over a cliff at Cherrapunji, Meghalaya, the wettest place on earth. The weather is often cloudy, since 450 inches of rain fall here each year.

The Northeastern States

In India's far northeast, in addition to Assam, there are six states and territories where travel is restricted. This is because of the area's strategic location between China, Burma, Bangladesh, and the rest of India, and because the region is troubled by local unrest and separatist movements. Hopefully, these regions will be made more accessible to travelers, because, with their forested hills and colorful tribespeople, they offer a wealth of natural and cultural beauty.

Meghalaya was separated from Assam in 1972 and is a hilly state inhabited by Garo, Khasi, and Jaintia tribespeople. The groups are largely Christian—they were converted by nineteenth–century missionaries—but are matrilineal and celebrate holidays with ancient folk dances. Shillong, the state capital, is a pleasant hill town. Cherrapunji is the world's wettest place, with 450 inches of rain each year. Not far away are monoliths commemorating ancestors.

Mountainous Arunachal Pradesh, north of Assam, borders China and is closed to visitors. Members of eighty–two Mongoloid and Tibeto–Burman tribes, mostly Buddhist, follow unique ways of life in this isolated state.

Nagaland takes its name from Naga tribespeople, who were fierce headhunters long ago. Naga warriors aided the British in the fight against Japanese invaders in 1943 and helped drive them back from Kohima, the farthest point west reached by the Japanese.

Manipur, on the Burmese border, is peopled by tribes related to the Shans of Burma. Manipuris are famous for their classical dance forms, yet are known as fierce fighters. In past centuries, they have engaged in hostilities with the Burmese, and more recently, helped repulse the Japanese.

Mizoram is bordered by Bangladesh on one side and Burma on the other. The Mizo tribespeople have been converted to Christianity, and literacy rates are high.

Tripura, a tiny state surrounded on three sides by Bangladesh, is home to several tribal groups related to Burmese tribes. It is a lush wooded region, with numerous beautiful waterfalls.

Viewed from Kaziranga, morning light shines on the snow–capped peaks of Arunachal Pradesh (Land of Dawn). Because of its proximity to the sensitive Chinese border, visitors can only glimpse the intriguing tribal region from afar.

The state of Meghalaya (Abode of Clouds) was separated from Assam in 1972. A hilly, foggy region, many of its tribal inhabitants are Christians. On misty hilltops, antique megaliths evoke the memories of tribal ancestors—upright stones for men and flatter stones for women.

A Naga tribesman of Nagaland displays his unique garb, including huge ivory armlets. His necklace suggests the Nagas' former head–hunting days, but his wristwatch ticks to modern time.

Tall ornate towers (gopurams) of Hindu temples testify to the faith of most South Indians. This four-hundred-year-old temple dedicated to Sri Virupaksha draws devotees at Hampi, Karnataka.

Golden ornaments studded with gems glimmer in the light of a votive oil lamp held by a lovely South Indian worshipper.

Scarlet turbans set off white clothing as a circle of South Indian men perform a vigorous round dance expressing social unity.

The Graceful South

There is a very special quality to South India. It shares many features of landscape and culture with the rest of India, yet the total ambience is somehow very distinctive, very much its own. Life seems more graceful, more pleasant, more traditional, and yet, in some places, more modern. The rice fields are lusher, the flowers brighter, the colors more vivid. Foreign influences have been strong—European colonizers and Muslim conquerors tried their best to make South India theirs—yet one cannot escape feeling that South India retains more of the essence of ancient, classical India than any other part of the country.

Southern India

The languages of the south belong to the Dravidian language family and are completely unrelated to the Indo–Aryan languages of most of the rest of India. Many believe that the original inhabitants of the Indus Valley civilization sites were Dravidian speakers. The people of Andhra Pradesh state speak Telugu; the people of Tamil Nadu speak Tamil; the inhabitants of Karnataka speak Kannada; and the people of Kerala speak Malayalam. Other languages are also spoken in certain regions—Tulu, Kodagi, and Yerava, among others. The cadence of these languages is entirely different from the rhythms of northern speech. Interestingly, however, many words of North Indian origin have been borrowed by Dravidian languages, particularly in matters of religion, and South Indian speech is thus graced by words of Sanskrit origin which connote great auspiciousness.

The colors of the South can be gorgeous. Against a backdrop of emerald rice paddies and palm trees, men in traditional white and women in shocking pink, lime green, royal blue, or citron yellow go about their daily lives. Women add shine to their lustrous black hair with coconut oil and adorn their long tresses with scarlet blossoms or snow–white jasmine. Against dark skin, gold jewelry flashes brightly. To bring good fortune into the home, white rice flour paste is used to create curvilinear rangoli designs on russet–toned earthen walls and doorsteps.

South Indian temples have their own distinctive architecture and atmosphere of devout Hinduism. Instead of the central temple spire of the north, here a temple is marked with a soaring gopuram, or gate tower, with a low central shrine. Some gateways are monumental rectangular pyramids completely encrusted with carvings of deities and mythical creatures. Walls and more gopurams enclose large temple complexes, sometimes almost like cities in their scope. Practices may be quite orthodox, and non–Hindus are often excluded from entering the inner sanctums of important temples. Priests and other Brahmans typically follow exacting standards of ritual purity and keep complex ancient rituals alive not only in temples but in their homes.

South Indian cuisines are elaborate and delicious. Rice preparations are essential, while delightful combinations of vegetables and spices enliven every meal. Fruits are abundant

The sacred Kaveri River springs from Brahmagiri Mountain in southwest Karnataka. Pilgrims often visit the holy Tala Kaveri (Head of the Kaveri) region, where they can worship as well as enjoy beautiful vistas.

Fisherfolk bend in unison to pull a fishing craft in from the sea at Goa, while foreign visitors stand by. Goa's beautiful beaches attract large numbers of visitors who enjoy the quiet peace of this lovely region.

The sun sets over the Arabian Sea at Goa, silhouetting a fisherman's boat resting on the soft sand.

and succulent. Each food has its special qualities of color, shape, texture, and taste which are taken into account in offering them to the deities, along with leaves, water, vermilion, flowers, and other auspicious substances. Life in South India is indeed a composition of great complexity, with many strains played by many instruments often blending together to create a beautiful and harmonious symphony.

Goa: Land of Balmy Beaches

For many visitors to India, Goa is their first introduction to the South. This tiny state was controlled by Portugal for 451 years before independent India decided to seize it in 1961. Goa is a delightful mixture of Indian and Iberian cultures set in an idyllic sun–washed landscape. The Konkani language is Indo–Aryan, with plenty of Dravidian mixed in. Most of the people are Hindu, but about a third are Christian. Portuguese surnames are common, and levels of education are high. Carnival is celebrated with great relish.

Spices and silks originally lured the Portuguese to these shores, and the prospect of saving souls drew missionaries like St. Francis Xavier. Baroque churches were built, and the Saint's body was enshrined in the Bom Jesus Basilica. Today, beautiful beaches and a light–hearted atmosphere attract foreign travelers seeking not material wealth but inner peace. In the shadow of the Iberians' houses of worship, today's gracious Goans smilingly tolerate tourists who ingest strange substances and do without clothes.

In the tiny town of Old Goa, the St. Francis of Assisi Church and Convent, built in 1661, represent the epitome of fine Portuguese architecture in India. The buildings' simple lines reflect the Franciscans' commitment to ordinary folk.

Karnataka: Protected by Deities

The large state of Karnataka is known for lush rice paddies, gentle hills, dry uplands, gushing waterfalls, and an extremely pleasant climate. Peopled by urbane city folk and hard–working villagers, the state is studded with ancient temples, ruined cities, and modern production plants as well as with palaces, gardens, and natural beauties. Here Hindu kingdoms held out against Muslim attackers, and Muslim rulers faced off against the British, while most of the population quietly continued to practice time–honored Hindu ways of life.

As in the rest of India, most people of Karnataka are engaged in making a living from the land. Here, rice is the main crop, with areca nut, cashews, vegetables, other grains, and spices also grown. Villagers dwell in carefully arranged settlements, following ritual practices which are very ancient in origin. In one rural region—probably quite typical—anthropologist Suzanne Hanchett has noted that as many as forty festivals are celebrated annually, all with a rich artistry of ceremony designed to please the gods and goddesses and solve human problems.

A gaur, a great wild ox, stands in the jungle at Nagarhole. Herds of more than twenty animals can sometimes be seen in this protected forest.

A herd of wild elephants forages in the forests and grasslands of Nagarhole National Park, Karnataka. Over a thousand of these huge beasts roam the area, one of the best remaining habitats for the Asian elephant.

Kuruba men are known for their skills in training elephants. In the mountainous forests of Coorg, this elephant helps move huge logs.

Snuggling a small child, Kuruba women bask in the sunshine outside their thatched forest home in southern Karnataka.

Bangalore and Mysore

Bangalore, Karnataka's capital, is a growing city of over three million, prominent as a center of science and industry as well as intelligent urban planning. Here are the Indian Institute of Science, Hindustan Aeronautics, Bharat Electronics, and other progressive institutions. Beautiful gardens are the verdant backdrops for parades of women in blossom–hued saris on their way, perhaps, to visit astrologers or to attend medical school classes.

A few miles outside Bangalore is the religious retreat of Satya Sai Baba, the renowned modern saint who materializes objects literally from thin air. Devotees come from all over India—and the world—to appeal to his wisdom and curative powers. Many of his followers are members of the intelligentsia.

Mysore City, once the royal capital of the Maharaja of Mysore, remains a city of palaces. The Mysore Palace dates from 1857 and is a marvelous confection of domes, arches, turrets, carvings, and chandeliers, often illuminated at night with thousands of tiny lights. Mysore, always a pleasant city, is at its best during the ten–day festival of Dassehra in September or October. Processions of royal elephants adorned in gold convey the splendor of the royal tradition as well as of the honored deities.

Outside of town are a huge Nandi, Shiva's holy bull, carved from a sixteen–foot block of granite; Brindavan Gardens, with gushing fountains dedicated to Krishna; and Srirangapatnam, an island fortress where Mysore rajas, the Muslim Hyder Ali, his son, the valiant Tipu Sultan, and, finally, in 1799, the British held sway. Under the British, power was restored to the old Hindu dynasty, whose royal descendant currently dwells in the Mysore Palace.

Royal elephants adorned for the ten–day Dassehra Festival pass through a palace gateway. Mysore's Dassehra festival pageantry, celebrating a goddess's victory over an evil demon, is spectacular.

The Maharaja's Palace at Mysore shines with thousands of tiny lights in celebration of the Dassehra Festival. The magnificent palace was built in 1857 in the Indo–Saracenic style, synthesizing Hindu and Islamic themes.

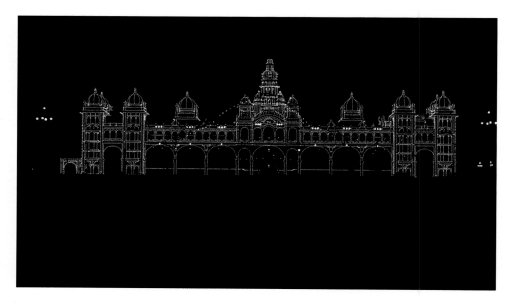

A waterfall refreshes the forest in the Coorg (Kodagu) region of southern Karnataka.

Preceding page:
A vista of the superb South Indian landscape spreads out before pilgrims going down the hill at Sravanbelgola after the bathing of Saint Gomateshwara's image.

An enormous image of the Jain Saint Gomateshwara has stood at Sravanbelgola for a thousand years. Every dozen years or so, thousands of pilgrims assemble to witness the spectacular bathing of the revered image with thousands of pots of holy water and other sacred substances.

On the outskirts of Bangalore, merchants and customers meet at a small market. Fruits, vegetables, and black earthenware pots are for sale.

Early Monuments

For ten centuries a huge image of a Jain saint has stood immobile atop a tall hill at Sravanbelgola. In fact, the statue of this naked saint Gomateshwara, for whom worldly goods meant nothing, is carved with creepers curling up his legs. So long did the saint stand in meditation that he was unaware of the passage of time. This enormous image, fifty–seven feet tall, carved from a single rock, is periodically the focus of a great pilgrimage. Once every twelve or fourteen years, many thousands of Jain pilgrims gather to participate in a ritual known as the mahamastakabhisheka. The saint's body is bathed with thousands of pots of water, milk, yogurt, butter, fruits, puffed rice, almonds, money, turmeric paste, and other auspicious substances. As the liquids gush over the huge image, pilgrims stand rapt in prayer. Boys brave the slosh at the base of the statue to dig out the coins. To have the privilege of witnessing this ancient ritual is to step back in time a thousand years.

Some of Karnataka's monuments date from even earlier times. At three lovely villages—Badami, Aihole, and Pattadakal—carved rock temples remain from the sixth to eighth centuries. There are lovely cave temples, hewn from solid rock, featuring Shiva, Vishnu, Jain saints, and loving couples, as well as a constructed temple to the Sun God and scores of other shrines.

The Hoysala Dynasty of A.D. 1000 to 1300, the first rulers to control all of the region now known as Karnataka, were great patrons of architecture and have left behind some remarkable temples. At Belur, Halebid, and Somnathpur, star–shaped temples are studded with superb sculptures depicting scenes from the Ramayana and the Mahabharata, as well as a variety of mythical and realistic figures. The carvings are of soft soapstone—which gradually hardens after it has been carved—allowing for the richest detail and the greatest proliferation of scenes and motifs in all of India. Some of the sculptures of women are voluptuously beautiful, adorned with carved stone bracelets and head ornaments that can actually be moved.

The Channakeshava temple at Belur, Karnataka, was constructed during the Hoysala Dynasty some eight hundred years ago. A high platform at the base of the temple provides a walkway for pilgrims making prayerful circumambulations of the star–shaped holy site while gazing at instructive sculptures.

Monsoon rains gush over a small shop along a Karnataka roadside. The inconvenience of the thunderous downpours is compensated for by the flourishing of life after the storms have cleared.

Incarnated as Narasimha, half–man/half–lion, Lord Vishnu tears a demon king to pieces. This ornate sculpture at the Hoysala temple at Halebid depicts the demise of an enemy who could be killed by neither man nor beast alone.

Vijayanagar

The wealthy Hindu kingdom of Vijayanagar stood as a bulwark against the challenge of Islamic invasion of South India for almost 250 years. From A.D. 1336 to 1565, the City of Victory held off invaders. Seven concentric walled citadels enclosed fields, pastures, water sources, and the city itself. Italian travelers of the fifteenth century reported that the king had twelve hundred concubines who accompanied him on litters wherever he went. A Muslim ambassador was awestruck by the splendor of the city and stressed the abundance of roses and pearls, rubies, emeralds, and diamonds. Portuguese ambassadors described the king dressed in white silk embroidered with gold roses, with a necklace of huge diamonds. One of his chambers was completely paneled in carved ivory. Elephants and horses were adorned in gold and gems, and ceremonies were dazzlingly impressive, involving thousands of retainers.

The king, however, was quite arrogant and encouraged his troops to defile Muslim shrines. As in most monarchies of the time, whether ruled by Muslim or Hindu kings, the common people were overtaxed to support the nobles, and punishments involved amputations, impalements, or being thrown to the elephants. In Vijayanagar, at the death of a noble, hundreds, or even thousands of wives and concubines were burned, so they would not outlive their lord. Finally, the combined armies of four Muslim kingdoms gathered to defeat their enemy and plunder the city. Today, the desolate ruined site at Hampi in Karnataka is proof of how temporary even the grandest of worldly majesty can be.

A temple chariot, complete with realistically turning wheels, was carved from a single stone at Vijayanagar, the great Hindu city of Karnataka. The city's heyday lasted from 1336 to 1565. It was then invaded by Muslim armies and fell to ruin.

Vijayanagar's domed elephant stables reflect Islamic architectural influence. Royal mounts to carry the king and his splendid retinue were quartered here. Today the site of the fabled city is known as Hampi.

A worker in Coorg removes leaves from drying coffee beans, a major commercial crop in the region. Tea is a favorite drink in North India, while coffee is the preferred beverage in much of the South.

Moplah Muslim men sit outside their colorful mosque in Coorg. Many Moplahs are descended from Arab traders who married local women. Some Moplah groups are matrilineal, while others are patrilineal.

Lovely Enclaves

Natural beauty, however, can last far longer. In the southernmost reaches of the state, among the wooded hills and grasslands of Nagarahole and Bandipur National Parks, wonderful glimpses of wildlife appear. Families of elephants, the wild gaur bison, deer, antelope, and even leopards and tigers can be seen amid superb scenery.

Also tucked into a mountainous southern corner of Karnataka is Coorg, once a separate princely state, but more recently ruled by the British. The Coorg people value their tradition of military service and are also very loyal to their families and traditional lands. Coffee is a major crop in this lovely upland region.

Andhra Pradesh: Rich Land and Kingdoms

Andhra Pradesh is the largest state in South India, both in area and in population. More than sixty-eight million people make this historically rich state their home. A beautiful coastline on the Bay of Bengal, fertile river valleys and deltas, forested hills, and vast plains provide varied environments for the nurturing of Telugu culture.

Reflecting differences in ecology and wealth, house types vary greatly from one region to another. Some houses are tiny round mud huts with pointed thatched roofs, while others are even smaller conical thatched sheds. In some regions, houses are constructed of stone, with slate shingles, and some have spacious interior courtyards affording protection and privacy. In rainy areas, pointed roofs are a must, while in dry areas, flat roofs are adequate. Thus, Andhra provides almost a complete sampling of the different kinds of houses to be found throughout India.

Most of the house types—and lives—of the ordinary people of Andhra Pradesh have probably retained their essential aspects over centuries, even as great historical forces mixed and clashed in this rich region. Villagers work in their fields and at their trades, quietly continuing their family and caste traditions. Visually prominent among Andhra people are the Banjaras, or Lambadis, whose Rajasthan-derived dress of mirror-studded scarlet adds brightness to the landscape.

On the occasion of a festival, Kuruba tribal laborers of Karnataka dress absurdly and dance raucously, calling out insults to their high-ranking employers. No offense can be taken during this special event.

Buddhist and Hindu Holy Places

At Nagarjunakonda, archaeologists have uncovered prehistoric artifacts as well as relics of a great Buddhist civilization that flourished during the third and fourth centuries. A great dam project was begun in 1954, and archaeologists worked to beat the clock before the area was flooded. By 1960, this historic area had disappeared beneath the lake created by the dam, but many fine treasures were saved. Among these was an elaborate reliquary with an innermost casket of gold encasing human bones, which an inscription attested were from Lord Buddha himself.

Nearby Amaravati was another ancient Buddhist center, supporting monasteries and a university that drew Buddhist scholars from as far away as China. While there is still much to see at this two-thousand-year-old site of the earliest and largest stupa in Andhra, it is painful to note that building contractors in search of construction stone vandalized the site some time ago. Further remnants were carted off to the Government Museum in Madras and the Victoria and Albert Museum in London. It is comforting, then, to consider that Sanchi, a similar site in Madhya Pradesh, while at one time ravaged by pothunters, has been thoughtfully restored to an admirable condition.

Their dress more colorful than that of the Rajasthanis they left behind generations ago, Banjara women gather to exchange news in their small village. Mirrorwork and distinctive huge earrings are worn even when these women work on construction projects.

A great many Hindu temples and forts bespeak the antiquity of the faith in Andhra. At Warangal stand four imposing gateways, which once gave entrance to a huge fort associated with Kakatiya Hindu rulers of the twelfth and thirteenth centuries. Nearby, a temple with a thousand pillars displays the low star-shaped design of the Hoysala temples of Karnataka. In Palampet, about forty miles from Warangal, the Kakatiyas built the Ramappa Temple, beautifully adorned with fascinating figures of wildlife, lotus blossoms, social activities, and six pairs of lovely female bracket figures, almost life-sized, sculptured from polished stone, their graceful bodies in a variety of dramatic poses. The Kakatiya kings also ordered the construction of a huge earth dam to control the water supply of the region.

Andhra's greatest tribute to Hinduism must surely be the great temple of Tirupati, one of India's favorite pilgrimage destinations. Since the days of the Pallava kings, over a thousand years ago, rulers have donated rich gifts to this hilltop temple. A sixteenth-century king presented the deity Sri Venkateswara with a jeweled crown, a gem-studded necklace, and twenty-five silver plates. Later, he donated thirty thousand gold coins. The tradition of lavish giving to the Tirupati Temple has continued to this day, and the temple is the wealthiest in all of India. Thousands of devotees offer not only money, gems, and precious metals, but also their hair. Often, a shaved head for a man or woman is the mark of a recent trip to Tirupati.

In Andhra Pradesh's Khammam District, a groom of the Banjara group prepares to claim his bride and depart from his in-laws' home after his wedding. Banjaras were originally wanderers from dry Rajasthan who came as traders and laborers to other parts of India, especially to Andhra.

Modern Hyderabad is a beehive of activity. The image of the late Rajiv Gandhi stands among those of politicians vying for public office in the elections of 1991. High above a statue of the ascetic Mahatma Gandhi are advertisements for television sets and fine fabric to be tailored into suits. A sign in cursive Telugu script is at right.

"There is no God but One, and Muhammad is his Prophet," declares a banner borne by Hyderabad Muslims at an event honoring an Islamic saint. Hyderabad has been a center of Islamic culture in South India for centuries.

Islam in Hyderabad

Even as Vijayanagar was a grand Hindu state, at the same time the Muslims were resplendent in the Bahmani kingdom just to the north. From 1347 to 1482, Muslim nobles enjoyed sumptuous living, supported by taxing the peasants, with harems including Muslim, Hindu, and European women. Urdu literature was cultivated in the courts of these Deccan Sultans—the court language was Dakhini Urdu, a southern version of the Indo–Aryan Muslim language of the north.

This empire disintegrated, and its territory was divided among five smaller Muslim kingdoms. Among these was the kingdom of Golconda, just five miles from the center of the city of Hyderabad, today's capital of Andhra Pradesh. The sprawling hilltop Golconda Fort was the seat of the Qutb Shahi dynasty for over 160 years. Among its rulers was Muhammad Quli Qutb Shah (1580–1611), regarded as one of the greatest of all Urdu poets. The wealth of the kingdom was legendary—its diamond mines produced the Hope Diamond and the Kohinoor Diamond—and the Mughal powers determined to have it for their own. Emperor Aurangzeb's forces besieged the fort and seized it through treachery in 1687. Its ruins today remind us of its time of glory.

Hyderabad city arose in 1590 and was the capital of the later offshoots of the Qutb Shahi dynasty, the Asaf Jahi Nizams, who ruled the largest kingdom in India until Indian independence. Here, the graceful Islamic culture of the South remained alive, patronized by the wealthy Nizams. The famed sixteenth–century Charminar building is a landmark of the modern city, fifth largest urban center in India. Its elegant arches and minarets combine elements of both Muslim and Hindu art, symbolizing the rich cultural fusion of the region.

Hyderabad also boasts the Salar Jung Museum, a fabulous collection of antiques and rare art treasures assembled by a twentieth–century prime minister of the Nizam's dominions. Modern Hyderabad is the center of a transport and communication network and is itself a great treasurehouse, marketing jewelry, crafts, grains, luscious fruits, and all of the wonders produced in South India today.

Tamil Nadu: Tower of Tradition

Tamil Nadu, formerly the state of Madras, is an incredible treasure trove of Indian tradition. The state covers much of the southeasternmost tip of the subcontinent, burgeoning with an abundance of temple art and the rich cultural complexity of South Indian life at its finest. Here Hinduism, Christianity, Islam, and Jainism have each contributed to the aromatic potpourri of Tamil tradition. Of special magnificence are the great Hindu temple complexes where priests, worshippers, metal casters, stoneworkers, dancers, florists, weavers, and merchants all play their part in maintaining ancient practices as vital parts of modern life. Brilliant festivals are celebrated with fervent feeling. Certainly, life has its vicissitudes, and the good things in life are far from equally distributed. Nonetheless, for more than fifty–seven million Tamils, life is shaped by valued ideals which have brought satisfaction for centuries.

Geographically, Tamil Nadu includes fertile plains glowing with brilliant green rice; white sandy beaches, where fisherfolk put out to sea; and misty forested uplands, where tribal people and wildlife dwell. Tamil women are especially active in rice cultivation, working in colorful groups to transplant the delicate shoots upon which human life depends. Men, too, work at tilling the soil and tending the crops, knowing that the failure of the rains can bring great hardship. Everywhere, as the people go about their daily lives, the presence of antique temples–some quiet monuments, others vibrant centers of worship–is a constant reminder of their ancient heritage.

In the Mylapore section of Madras, the Kapaleswara Temple dedicated to Lord Shiva is a riot of color. During a dry spell, bathing steps lead down to an empty bathing tank. The popular temple was built in the 1600s, and its bright colors are frequently refreshed.

Bending low over a muddy rice paddy, these women know that their own well–being depends greatly on that of the seedlings they so carefully transplant. The verdure of Tamil Nadu's rice fields depends greatly on women's work.

Madras and Mahabalipuram

Madras, Tamil Nadu's capital, is the fourth largest city in India, after Calcutta, Bombay, and Delhi. This coastal center of trade has drawn traffic from all over the world for centuries and maintains a cosmopolitan quality as well as a Tamil air. The center of South India's film industry, its skyline is ablaze with bright movie billboards advertising the latest celluloid fantasies. Many movie stars have gone on to political fame, their roles as mythical heroes in historic dramas standing them in good stead with the voters.

The British arrived here early, building Fort St. George in 1640, the nucleus of today's city. The fort withstood onslaughts from Indian and French attackers, and some of its buildings still stand as reminders of English aspirations in India. The British found Christianity well established here, apparently having been brought to India by the Apostle St. Thomas in the first century. The apostle's remains are said to be entombed at San Thome Church.

Another important house of worship is the Kapaleswara Shiva Temple at Mylapore in Madras. Its ornate gopuram tower is a riot of color, matched only by the vivid saris of worshippers at the three–hundred–year–old temple. The Government Museum displays fine bronzes of Hindu deities created by artisans of the Chola period (ninth through thirteenth centuries) which bespeak the devotions of the time, so similar to those of today.

A few miles south of Madras, at Mahabalipuram, on the sandy shores of the Bay of Bengal, a beautiful group of rock–cut monuments evokes the past. Seventh–century carvings of the Pallava dynasty include a series of freestanding boulders carved to resemble small temples and animals. Rock–cut caves and a masterful stone bas–relief are nearby. The "Penance of Arjuna" relief, cut on two huge rocks, shows scores of figures of deities, people, and animals, including, according to one interpretation, the emaciated figure of Arjuna, the great warrior of the Mahabharata, standing on one leg and doing penance, praying to Lord Shiva for the strength to destroy his enemies. Sadhus of today perform this exact act of sacrificial devotion. On the adjacent beach stands one of South India's oldest temples, the Shore Temple, its foundations washed for twelve centuries by the frothy sea.

A fire–breathing professional street performer impresses onlookers in Madras. Part of a traveling troupe, he balances an auspicious decorated vessel on his head.

Dancers of the classical Bharat Natyam dance form rehearse ancient steps at their Mylapore home. Originally developed in South Indian temples, Bharat Natyam is now performed before appreciative secular audiences.

Celestial light shines on fisherman on the sea near Madras. Their long boat is powered with a large oar.

South of Madras, at Mahabalipuram, one of India's oldest temples stands beside the sea. The Shore Temple has withstood the washing of the waves since the eighth century.

Tiny elephants protected between the legs of a large tusker—as well as other animals, spirits, and deities of every kind—are represented in the huge stone bas–relief at Mahabalipuram. The carving is commonly known as Arjuna's Penance, after the figure of an emaciated ascetic standing on one foot, presumably the mythic hero Arjuna praying to Lord Shiva for strength to defeat his enemies.

Other incredible carvings at Mahabalipuram include representations of several very early temple styles cut from solid granite boulders in the seventh century.

179

Great Temple Towns

Far to the south, inland, is Madurai, a lively temple center where medieval scenes of faith are enacted daily. With its ornate architecture and throngs of worshippers, Madurai has been called the "heart of Tamil country" and provides all visitors, Hindu and non–Hindu, with indelible impressions.

Shiva and his wife, in the form of Meenakshi, are honored in Madurai's great Meenakshi Temple. Giant gopuram towers are ornamented with a profusion of deities, all painted in brilliant colors. Inside the walls of the complex are a bathing tank and a Hall of a Thousand Pillars, each carved with fascinating figures. Two sanctuaries shelter Shiva and his wife, where thousands of daily worshippers crowd to offer foods and flowers to the holy beings. In the outer pillared courtyards, trumpets, drums, and chants resound, and the statues of lesser deities also receive attention—devotees pour oil and even throw blobs of butter on them in attempts to please the gods and goddesses. One's relationship with the Divine, often privately expressed in the West, is here openly displayed with poignantly fervent emotion.

There are scores of other great temple towns in India, each with its own history and fabulously carved religious architecture, perhaps the greatest achievement of Tamil civilization. The names are redolent with history and tradition–Kanchipuram, the Golden City of Temples, studded with towering shrines and workshops of weavers producing vividly colored silks; Thiruvannamalai; Chidambaram, where ancient temple walls display sculptures of dance forms still practiced by Bharat Natyam performers; Thanjavur, home of a Shiva Temple regarded by some as India's greatest temple; Tiruchirapalli, with a high rock fort and temple complex; Srirangam, a great walled temple on an island in the Kaveri River; Rameshwaram on the far southern coast, with its tall tower and sculptured corridors, the longest in the world; and finally, Kanya Kumari, at Cape Cormorin, itself a naturally holy spot by virtue of its location at the very southern tip of the subcontinent, where the Bay of Bengal, the Indian Ocean, and the Arabian Sea all flow together, mixing the waters of the sacred oceans.

A Brahman priest and his wife worship the Sun God in the courtyard of their home at Madurai. Ritual offerings of flowers and foods are carefully arranged according to a complex symbolic system. Auspicious plants grow in decorated containers. The purpose of the ritual is to maintain human harmony with divine forces, thus allowing the family and human society to flourish.

Ten giant gopuram towers beckon the faithful to worship at the Meenakshi Temple in Madurai, one of Hinduism's busiest centers. Madurai is considered the heart of Tamil country.

A saffron–robed holy man walks past a temple wall in Madurai. Red and white stripes are a common feature of South Indian temple walls, symbolically alternating heating and cooling forces of the cosmos to produce a harmonious balance in nature and human life.

Laborers bend to the task of winnowing rice at a threshing floor near Madurai, Tamil Nadu. Rice is South India's staff of life.

The Pallava kings, who built Mahabalipuram's monuments, had their capital at Kanchipuram. This Golden City of Temples contains more than a hundred significant shrines. Here a sacred bull flanked by lions faces a Shiva temple of the eighth century.

The Nilgiri Hills

Mention must be made of the exquisite beauty of the Nilgiris—the Blue Hills—of inland Tamil Nadu. These peaceful uplands, shrouded in cooling mists, are home to the unique Toda tribe, herders of sacred buffalo. The men wear beards and the women long curls. Both wrap themselves in intricately embroidered togalike robes. The Todas' traditional homeland at Ootacamund is now heavily planted in tea and coffee, and urban folk enjoy visiting here to breathe cool air and play golf and tennis. Still, the Todas continue their traditions, some still living in their singular barrel–shaped houses, reminiscent of the rock–carved halls at Ajanta and the distinctive temples of Assam.

High in Tamil Nadu's Nilgiri Hills (Blue Hills), women pluck tea leaves from cultivated bushes on a tea plantation. Nilgiri–grown tea is considered to be among the world's finest.

On the festival of Mattu Pongal in Tamil Nadu, a running of the bulls occurs which is similar to bull running in Pamplona, Spain. Specially reared animals are decorated with rupee notes, scarves, and flower garlands. Some even have their horns sharpened.

Young men reach out to a bull running through the crowd. Honor goes to those who successfully ride the bull and wrest the money from his head. Some who try are seriously gored or trampled by the bulls. This celebration was held in Aranganalur, a village near Madurai.

Kerala: Where Cultures Meet

When one thinks of a tropical paradise with white sand beaches shaded by waving palms, one is thinking of Kerala. Here boats loaded with coconut husks are poled down inland waterways past verdant banks of foliage dotted with white–walled homes. Balmy breezes ruffle the skirts of girls walking to school along palm–lined footpaths. In village ponds, elephants are bathed by their handlers, and in green fields, rice is tended by diligent farmers. Amid the luxuriant foliage, one can glimpse the spires of Hindu temples, Muslim mosques, and Christian churches. Sheltered in a cozy town street there is even a synagogue. Life in Kerala can be lovely.

In this small state on India's southwesternmost coast, nearly thirty million crowded people seek contentment. Many decide to go elsewhere; Kerala exports large numbers of people—nurses, teachers, scholars, and doctors—to all parts of the globe. In recent years, many workers have gone to work in the oil–rich Gulf States, sending their salaries home to pay for cement houses and loud television sets.

Actually, it is nothing new for Kerala to look outward—the world has been coming to this region for perhaps three thousand years. The spicy treasures of the Malabar Coast (now Kerala)—including pungent black pepper and fragrant cardamom, along with other items of trade—attracted Phoenicians, Arabs, Jews, Chinese, Dutch, Portuguese, French, and British. The Zamorin of Calicut greeted Portugal's Vasco da Gama in 1498, little suspecting how greedy the Europeans would eventually show themselves to be.

Kerala's literacy rate is the highest of any state in India—ninety–one percent versus fifty–two percent for the country. Political consciousness is high: Kerala freely elected a communist state government decades ago. Women's status is high also, and, as medical care has improved, family planning is favored. Kerala is home to the unique Nayar people—traditionally matrilineal. In times past, women remained in their ancestral homes after marriage, with peripatetic husbands visiting as desired. Here, too, Nambudiri Brahmans followed distinctive customs of marriage and lifestyle. For both Nayars and Nambudiris, customs are now changing, but Kerala's proud sense of uniqueness remains strong.

Christianity came early to Kerala–St. Thomas is said to have brought it in A.D. 50, and Kerala Christians form a prestigious community. About a quarter of Kerala's people are Christian. The Jews arrived here even earlier–supposedly in the sixth century B.C., followed by a bigger wave in the first century, when the Romans were persecuting them.

The Pooram temple festival at Trichur is a fantastic event, complete with processions of elephants adorned with gold ornaments. The elephant in the center carries the image of Lord Vadakkumnathan around the temple complex. Curved trumpets sound, and colorful displays of fireworks brighten the night.

The Jewish community in Kerala traces its earliest arrivals in India to the sixth century B.C. The Cochin synagogue dates from 1568 and is adorned with fine glass lamps and floor tiles. Hindu kings of cosmopolitan Kerala extended their welcome to early Jewish immigrants.

A Kathakali dancer at Cochin displays his elaborate performance make–up and costume. Spectacular Kathakali dance–dramas portray scenes from the Hindu epics through highly stylized motions.

Bursting with energy, team members paddle a high–sterned snake–boat at an exciting race on a palm–fringed canal at Alleppey.

Palm trees line a canal in Kerala, India's uniquely tropical southwestern state. In verdant Kerala, water is everywhere, and people often bathe twice a day. Boats loaded with coconuts and coconut husks are poled down inland waterways on their way to markets outside the state.

They found a warm welcome in tolerant Kerala (until the Portuguese got involved many centuries later). Their present synagogue at Cochin dates from 1568 and is adorned with Chinese tiles. Many of India's Jews have departed for economic opportunity in Israel, and the population is dwindling.

Worship at Kerala's Hindu temples can be inspiring, as at Trivandrum's great house of worship, when hundreds of tiny coconut oil lamps are lit in the dark of the evening. Colorful kathakali dance dramas are a delightful feature of Kerala Hindu religious life. Costumes and makeup are spectacular, reminiscent of Chinese opera. Elephants are everywhere—both wild, as at Periyar Wildlife Sanctuary, and domestic, hauling logs in the jungle, or parading in golden regalia at the Pooram festival procession at Trichur. Onam, Kerala's great harvest festival, is celebrated with colorful circular mosaics of brilliant blossoms and thrilling snake–boat races with lithe oarsmen in energetic competition on Kerala's palm–fringed canals.

Fantasy Islands

Some two hundred to four hundred miles west of Kerala's coast are scattered the islands of Lakshadweep, sometimes called the Laccadive Islands. This coral archipelago supports some fifty–two thousand people with coconut farming and fishing. The crystalline waters provide opportunities to view colorful corals and fish, and beaches are uncrowded. In the opposite direction, 850 miles to the east of mainland India's coast, are the Andaman and Nicobar Islands, home to a number of aboriginal tribes. Some of these groups accept contact with outsiders, but at least one group has used bows and arrows to discourage visitors.

India includes the far–flung island territories of Lakshadweep—the Laccadive Islands—to the west, and the Andaman and Nicobar Islands to the east. Here, at Kavaratti in Lakshadweep, a beautiful beach beckons.

As it descends, the sun is caught in a Chinese fishing net at Cochin. The net is lowered and raised by means of levered poles.

Index of Photographers

Index by Photographer

Index by Page

The sun sets behind the Shore Temple at Mahabalipuram, as it has done for over twelve hundred years. With such wonders all around them, India's children learn much about the past as they move forward to meet the challenges of the future.

Afterword

In every village, every town, and every region of India, one sees a highly complex and ancient civilization at work. Great architecture, fine crafts, beautiful art, complicated systems of agriculture and social organization, inspired religions, magnificent festivals—all are part of daily life for the people of India. Today's Indians can freely draw upon their deeply rooted heritage as they shape new institutions with which to meet the future. People living today share love and hope with one another, and they also share with the many generations of the past the most heartfelt ambition to create whole and satisfying lives for themselves and for their children within the embrace of the land of India.